A Green Witch's G to Herbal Medicine:

How to Identify, Forage, and Craft Powerful Natural Remedies

by Sage Willowbrook

ᎤᎻᎾᏆᏆᎷ ᏞᏞᎾᎸᎻᏛᏚ ᎲᎾᎦᎢᎥᏏ ᎷᏏ ᎢᏆᎻᏅᏕᎦ ᏪᏆᎻᎤᏔᎤᏂᏆ᎓ ᎢᎻᏅᏅ
ᏛᏆ ᎢᎾᏆᏂᏛᎤᎦᎷ ᎢᏆᎻᏆᎤᏆ ᎢᏂᎻ ᏔᎻᏆᏆᏛ ᏐᎷᏅᏆᏆᎻᏞᏅ ᏂᏔᏛᎦᎻᏆᏃ
ᎷᏆᏆᎻᎷᎤᏔᏛ ᏅᏃ ᏛᎢᎤᏆ ᏞᏞᎤᏃᏃᎻᏞᏛᎷᎷᏆᏏ

"Spirits of nature, I honor your presence, and ask for your guidance as I walk my path, respecting all life and cherishing the Earth's abundance."

A Green Witch's Guide to Herbal Medicine: By Sage Willowbrook
Published by Chek Publishing

Printed in United States of America
First Edition

TABLE OF CONTENTS

BEWITCHING BEGINNINGS

An Introduction to Green Witchery in Herbal Healing

"Great spirits of the Earth, guide me in my actions to live in harmony with all creation, nurturing the world as it nurtures me."

Beneath the vast, echoing dome of the sky and cradled in the verdant heart of the earth, the spirit of the Green Witch stirs and awakens. The Green Witch is a figure not of myth or lore, but of reality, of intimate connection to the natural world. The forest's hush, the rustle of leaves underfoot, and the ceaseless hum of life all around become the symphony to which the Green Witch dances. For them, the Earth is not just a giver of resources to be utilized, but a living entity, a mother, a teacher, and a friend.

This bond between the Green Witch and the natural world transcends our conventional understanding of nature as just a provider. It delves deeper, recognizing Earth as a breathing canvas of life, energy, and wisdom. As Green Witches, we see ourselves not as separate from this canvas but as a part of it, painting our own strokes of existence along with every plant, every creature, every element.

In this book, "A Green Witch's Guide to Herbal Medicine," we pay homage to the abundant richness of the Earth and the nurturing arms of nature. It's more than a journey; it's an immersion into the vibrant heart of the natural world. It's a deep dive into the realm of medicinal plants, the inherent wisdom of the Earth, and the ethereal spirit that binds all life together.

Our ancestors knew the Earth in a way many of us have forgotten. They understood her rhythms, her whispers, her secrets. They were the original Green Witches, drawing on the wisdom of the Earth to heal, to thrive, to live. From the ancient Sumerians, who inscribed the healing properties of over 250 different plants on clay tablets, to our primate relatives, bonobos and chimpanzees, who instinctively seek out certain plants for their medicinal virtues, the Earth has offered her wisdom generously to all who would listen.

Being a Green Witch goes beyond knowing the properties of plants and how to use them. It's about fostering a symbiotic relationship with nature, understanding and respecting her rhythms and cycles, honoring her gifts, and recognizing her hand in our existence. As we explore the realm of herbal medicine, we'll be guided by this principle, learning not just to use nature but to commune with her.

This book is your key to unlock the secrets of the natural world. Within its pages, you will learn to forage with the intuition of a Green Witch, identify the healing plants that thrive around us, and craft natural remedies potent with the Earth's energy. It's more than just a guide; it's an invitation to step into a world where the spiritual and the physical intertwine, where the magic of nature is a tangible, healing force.

Embrace the path of the Green Witch. Let the wisdom of the Earth guide you on a journey of holistic healing, of spiritual growth, and of a return to our roots. As you turn each page, may your bond with the Earth deepen, and may her wisdom, her strength, and her energy become a part of you. Welcome to the world of the Green Witch, a world where nature is not just observed but lived, not just respected but revered. Let's begin this journey together.

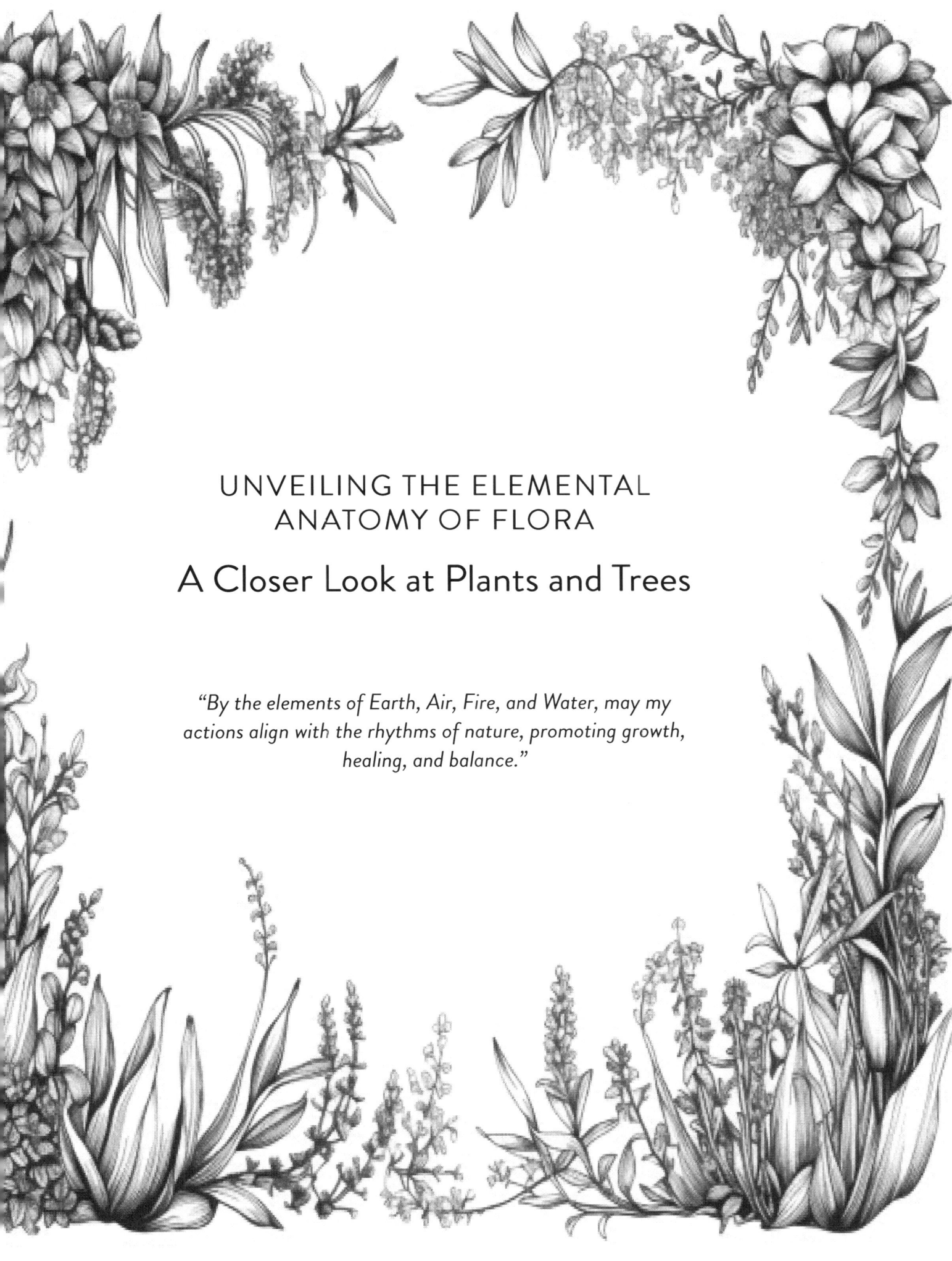

UNVEILING THE ELEMENTAL ANATOMY OF FLORA

A Closer Look at Plants and Trees

"By the elements of Earth, Air, Fire, and Water, may my actions align with the rhythms of nature, promoting growth, healing, and balance."

For every Green Witch, there is a journey that awaits, a journey steeped in wisdom and knowledge, understanding, and deep connection. This journey takes you, the inquisitive witch, straight into the embrace of nature, allowing you to wander amidst a plethora of flora, unlocking their profound secrets one by one. As you immerse yourself in this fascinating world, you develop the unique skill of foraging, honing the ability to conscientiously and respectfully gather plants and various parts of trees, seamlessly integrating them into your daily life and sacred spaces.

As you weave the wisdom of the Green Witch into the fabric of your life, foraging becomes less of a simple task and more of an intrinsic ritual. Your footprints mark the path to nature's abundant treasures, where you learn to identify and gather plants and trees that mirror your needs, desires, and intentions. For some, the thrill of this journey lies in finding wild, edible treasures that nature generously provides. For others, it's a double delight to unearth not only culinary delights but also medicinal wonders hidden within the verdant expanses. Regardless of the specifics, the essence of the foraging ritual is identical for every Green Witch. It is a dance that begins with stepping into the wilderness, continues with the identification of flora, and culminates in the respectful collection of plants.

Your ability to excel in this sacred ritual depends largely on your grasp of plant and tree anatomy. The ability to identify and differentiate the various parts of plants, to understand their unique energies and properties, becomes a vital milestone on your journey as a Green Witch. This knowledge serves a dual purpose—it offers enlightenment and understanding, yes, but it also acts as a safeguard, a necessary precautionary measure. The story of the wild black cherry tree, an ordinary plant bearing complex secrets, provides a telling example of this dichotomy.

My own interaction with this tree is a tale worth sharing. In the heart of my yard, unnoticed and unappreciated for years, stood a regal wild black cherry tree. Its identity remained shrouded in mystery, and the resources it offered went unrecognized. When I finally unveiled its true identity, a sense of awe enveloped me. Yet, the tree held further secrets—the leaves, stems, and fallen branches were home to hydrocyanic acid, a compound that transforms into lethal cyanide when damaged or deceased.

Armed with this newfound knowledge, I approached the tree with respect and caution, carefully harvesting its fragrant outer bark. I prepared an infusion from it, sweetened with the soothing touch of honey. What resulted was a potent, homemade cough remedy and calming aid, a powerful testimony to the tree's healing prowess. This experience underscored an essential truth—knowing how to identify and understand the diverse parts of a plant can dramatically shape your interactions with nature. Such understanding can lead to remarkable, often life-altering outcomes.

As we delve deeper into our journey of botanical discovery, it's time to become better acquainted with the fundamental components of any plant. They form the core of our understanding and interaction with the green world and will be the stepping stones on our path to becoming adept Green Witches.

Roots

Serving as life's anchors, roots burrow deep into the earth, absorbing vital nutrients to nourish the plant. A true treasure trove of plant chemistry, roots often house an array of medicinal properties that have been harnessed for centuries. Simultaneously, they offer sustenance, with their starchy composition providing a hearty source of nutrition. Yet, their high concentration of bioactive compounds can sometimes tip the balance towards toxicity. As such, accuracy in root identification is essential for safe and effective use.

Stems

The bridge connecting the earth and sky, stems are the plant's lifeline, responsible for transporting water, nutrients, and sugars between roots and leaves. While they often play a secondary role in our interactions with plants, there are notable exceptions. Plants like echinacea, for instance, hold medicinal virtues not just in their colorful blooms but also in their robust stems, making every part of the plant a valuable resource. The first thing to emerge from the dirt is going to be the stems. Some plants have long, and substantial stems and others have very short and frail stems that give way to dominant leaves. Either way the part of the plant that protrudes from the ground is always the stem.

Leaves

The green engines of life, leaves are the plant's food factories, synthesizing sunlight into nourishment through photosynthesis. They also serve as repositories of potent bioactive compounds, making them integral to both culinary and medicinal uses. Think of the humble tea leaf, which transforms into a health-boosting brew, or the fragrant herbs that elevate our culinary creations. The potential held within each leaf is immense, making it a significant part of a Green Witch's materia medica.

Flowers

Serving as the plant's reproductive hub, flowers hold a unique charm. Their beauty often belies their power, with many blossoms harboring potent medicinal properties. Be it the iconic dandelion or the less conspicuous elderberry, each flower carries its unique essence and healing potential. Recognizing these often fleeting floral wonders is crucial for any Green Witch aiming to harness their gifts.

Fruits

The culmination of the plant's reproductive process, fruits house the seeds that carry the promise of future generations. Despite their purpose of ensuring the plant's continuity, fruits also play a pivotal role in herbalism. Their diverse forms—from succulent apples and cherries to simple seed pods—carry their own medicinal properties, contributing to the wide array of remedies available to the skilled Green Witch. Recognizing the fruits borne by plants is a rewarding skill, one that ensures a fruitful (pun intended) foraging experience.

Remember, a Green Witch's journey doesn't stop at mere identification. It involves understanding each plant's intricate components, unraveling the complex chemistry contained within, and using this wisdom to create potent remedies. By nurturing this symbiotic relationship with nature, you become a true custodian of the green world, ensuring its gifts are respected, utilized, and preserved for generations to come.

UNLEASHING THE GREEN WITCH WITHIN

Embracing Your Forager Spirit and the Tools You'll Need

"Sacred Earth, in your grounding embrace, inspire me to nurture and protect all life, as I am but a leaf on the great tree of existence."

As a Green Witch, you are innately a forager. This is not merely a fleeting interest or a hobby to dabble in during your free time. Instead, it is an integral part of who you are, an extension of your connection with nature, and a crucial aspect of your craft.

We could argue that deep within us, the essence of the forager has always been present. As we've traced back through history, we've seen the intrinsic role of foraging in our ancestors' lives. The brief period in our timeline where foraging has been replaced by a trip to the local supermarket is but an aberration, a deviation from our true nature.

Now, to harness the full potential of your forager spirit, you'll need some tools to aid your journey. These tools, carefully crafted from metal, embody a perfect blend of ancient wisdom and modern ingenuity. They stand far superior to the simple implements of our forebears and can significantly enhance your foraging endeavors.

However, remember that these tools are not mere ornaments or symbols of your path. They hold their power in their use, not in their mere possession. As a committed forager, don't let these tools gather dust on a shelf. Instead, let them become an extension of your hands, an integral part of your interaction with the natural world.

Below, I present a list of indispensable foraging tools. They're not exotic or hard to find; in fact, most can be procured from your local hardware store. These tools are your companions on your journey, helping you engage with the flora around you in a meaningful and transformative way.

Tool List

The Power of the Ounce Scale

In the path of a Green Witch, tools for harvesting wild medicine are essential, but so are the tools used in the more delicate, subtle aspects of our practice. One such tool is the ounce scale. It may not be employed in the heart of the wilderness, but when it comes to concocting tinctures and determining doses of your carefully crafted herbal remedies, its role is indispensable.

Choosing your scale is a personal matter, influenced by your individual circumstances and preferences. Many Green Witches appreciate the convenience of a digital scale. Its ease of use and compact size are indeed advantageous. However, relying on such a device means you'll have to ensure it remains powered. And if your inclination towards wild medicine stems from a vision of societal collapse or supply chain disruption, keeping a steady supply of batteries for your digital scale may prove challenging.

On the other hand, you might consider a traditional mechanical scale, perhaps a robust receiving scale with 1- or 2-ounce increments. Such a scale operates independently of electricity, allowing you to weigh your medicinal herbs and plants even in the face of a power outage or more extended grid down scenario. This choice ensures you can continue your Green Witch practices undisturbed, regardless of what the world around you is facing.

In either case, possessing a reliable ounce scale will be a necessity for the numerous preparations and practices outlined in this book. It ensures precision and consistency in your craft, traits highly valued by any Green Witch.

Harvesting with Care: The Essential Small Shovel

As you begin to connect with the plant world on a more profound level, you'll soon realize that the roots of many wild herbs and medicinal plants hold tremendous power. They are potent repositories of nutrients and plant-based compounds, often housing the concentrated essence of the plant's healing capabilities. To access these buried treasures, the small shovel becomes your indispensable ally.

This humble tool, simple yet highly effective, empowers you to delve beneath the surface and retrieve the medicinal bounty the earth has nurtured. With a small spade in hand, you can carefully excavate around the root ball, ensuring you cause minimal disruption to the surrounding soil and plant life. Its compact size ensures precision, allowing you to extract what you need without unnecessary damage or waste.

This mindful approach to harvesting, facilitated by the use of a small shovel, reflects the essence of the Green Witch's creed – to interact with nature with respect, gratitude, and a conscious intent to preserve and protect. As you gather your roots, remember that your actions influence the equilibrium of the ecosystem. The small shovel, then, is not just a tool, but a symbol of your commitment to sustainable and respectful foraging.

The Power of the Digging Fork: For the Root Seeker

While a small shovel proves to be a reliable companion for most root excavation tasks, certain scenarios call for a tool with a little more muscle and precision - the digging fork. Tailor-made for the job, a digging fork is your go-to instrument when the task at hand is to extract the smaller, often elusive, roots that lie beneath the surface of the earth.

The digging fork is robust and sturdy, its sturdy tines designed to penetrate the soil deeply and efficiently. With this in hand, you can confidently engage in the meticulous task of unearthing smaller roots without causing them harm or damage. It provides the perfect balance of strength and delicacy needed to navigate the complex network of roots beneath the surface.

But remember, the digging fork is a heavy tool. It requires careful handling and should only be brought along on your foraging journey when you're specifically targeting root harvesting. The weight it adds to your foraging kit is justified by its efficiency and precision in bringing those invaluable medicinal roots into your possession.

Like every tool in your Green Witch arsenal, the digging fork symbolizes your connection with the earth and your dedication to ethical and sustainable foraging practices. As you wield it, let it be a reminder of your role as a steward of the earth, a guardian of nature's secrets, and a respectful extractor of her medicinal gifts.

Meet the Hori Hori: A Multitool Born of History

One tool that truly encapsulates the essence of the Green Witch's craft, blending practicality, history, and a bit of mystique, is the Hori Hori. This Japanese gardening multitool, appearing more like a sizeable, fixed-blade knife than a traditional trowel, is a must-have asset in your foraging kit.

The genesis of the Hori Hori is steeped in historical resilience and adaptability. In 1876, during the Meiji era, the Japanese government placed a ban on the creation of Katanas, the revered weapon of the Samurai. This momentous decision meant that the swordsmiths, masters in forging the magnificent Samurai swords, found their craft outlawed overnight. However, their skills and creativity were far from extinguished. The birth of the Hori Hori was a testament to their ingenuity as they pivoted from crafting weaponry to designing kitchen and garden tools, and in the process, creating a multitool that has withstood the test of time.

The Hori Hori is uniquely designed, with each side sporting a different edge. One side features a serrated edge, ideal for pruning and cutting through tough plant materials. The other side offers a straight edge, perfect for slicing greens and other delicate tasks. This dual-edged approach makes the Hori Hori a versatile tool, capable of performing multiple tasks with ease, from digging to cutting, and everything in between.

But beyond its practicality, the Hori Hori carries with it a legacy of transformation and versatility, encapsulating the essence of what it means to adapt, to persevere, and to continue blooming even amidst challenges. And as a Green Witch, this is a lesson and energy you carry into your own interactions with the natural world. Thus, the Hori Hori is not just a tool, but a symbol of the resilient spirit within you.

Kitchen Shears: Gentle Touch for Delicate Harvests

As you immerse yourself in the world of foraging, you'll soon realize that not all herbs and plants demand heavy-duty tools. Indeed, many medicinal plants are delicate and only require a gentle touch. In these instances, a trusty pair of kitchen shears can be your best ally.

Just imagine standing amidst a wild patch of chamomile or rosemary. These plants, with their soft, delicate stems, don't need the force of a sharp blade. Rather, a gentle snip with kitchen shears can harvest them efficiently without causing unnecessary damage. Even more robust herbs, like basil or mint, can benefit from the clean cut provided by these scissors, preserving their integrity and freshness.

One of the benefits of using kitchen shears for your foraging excursions is their ubiquity. Most likely, you already have a pair at home. Why not incorporate them into your foraging toolkit? They are lightweight, easily portable, and often feature comfortable handles, making them ideal for extended foraging sessions.

Remember, being a Green Witch is about fostering a respectful relationship with nature. Using tools like kitchen shears that can minimize harm to the plants aligns with this ethos. So, before you embark on your next foraging journey, consider packing your kitchen shears. You'll find they're a surprisingly versatile tool, offering a tender touch for your delicate harvests.

Pruning Saw: The Mighty Companion for Robust Harvests
Venturing deeper into the foraging practice, you'll inevitably encounter the need to prune larger hardwood trees for their bark - a valuable resource in many medicinal preparations. In these situations, the strength of your toolkit must rise to the occasion. Enter the pruning saw, a robust tool designed to handle the challenges of thick tree branches and tough bark.

Picture this: amidst your explorations, you come across a mature willow tree, its bark known for its pain-relieving properties. To harvest this bark ethically and efficiently, you'll need a tool that can handle the rigidity of the mature tree. That's where a pruning saw comes into play.

My go-to choice is a simple folding saw from my camping gear. With an 8-inch blade, it might seem modest, but don't be fooled. This compact tool is a workhorse, capable of sawing through sizeable branches with ease. Its folding design makes it perfect for safe transport, and it won't weigh down your foraging bag.

The pruning saw exemplifies the essence of a good foraging tool: robust, reliable, and respectful to nature. It allows you to take what you need without causing unnecessary harm to the tree, honoring the balance between humans and nature. So, as you prepare for your next foraging journey, consider equipping yourself with a pruning saw. You'll find it an indispensable ally when faced with the sturdier specimens of the plant kingdom.

Pruners: Precision Cutters for the Green Witch

As a Green Witch, precision is as crucial as efficiency when engaging with the world of wild plants. That's why pruners - the agile cutters of your foraging tool kit - should not be overlooked. These tools excel where others might falter, especially when faced with the woody stems of many wild edibles.

Picture yourself on a foraging expedition, coming across a dense patch of woody stemmed herbs - maybe wild rosemary or sagebrush, each with their myriad of medicinal benefits. Here, the kitchen shears may struggle, and while the hori hori can manage, it may not provide the clean, swift cut you need to preserve the plant's vitality. That's where pruners prove their worth.

Pruners are designed to cut through thicker stems with minimal effort, providing a clean, quick cut that minimizes damage to the plant and ensures a healthier harvest. They're more than just a convenience; they're a way of showing respect to the plants you're working with. With a simple squeeze, you can gather your desired plant parts, leaving the rest of the plant unharmed and able to continue its growth.

Having a reliable set of pruners in your foraging arsenal is like having a masterful, sharp-edged ally. They allow you to navigate the wild plant world with finesse, enabling a seamless interaction between your witchy aspirations and the nature that supports them. So remember, whether it's to snip through a tough stem or to secure a clean harvest, never underestimate the power of a good set of pruners.

Survival Knife: A Full-Tang Companion for your Woodland Ventures
When you, as a Green Witch, embark on a foraging journey into the heart of the woods, a full-tang survival knife proves to be an essential companion. This trusty tool, residing within easy reach on your belt, emerges as a versatile asset that compliments your woodland endeavors and fortifies your foraging toolkit.

Imagine yourself deep in the forest, surrounded by the songs of birds and rustle of leaves. Your eyes wander, appreciating the serenity and raw beauty nature offers, and then they land on a promising plant - an elderberry bush or a burdock, perhaps. A swift glance reveals that harvesting some parts of these plants could be a bit tricky. That's where your survival knife steps into the spotlight.

Not just a blade, a full-tang survival knife embodies versatility and durability, boasting a blade that extends the full length into the handle. This design provides strength and stability - qualities you'd want when you're deep in the forest, interacting with nature in its rawest form. It becomes an invaluable companion, capable of serving multiple functions beyond just cutting.

Whether it's digging up roots, cutting through thicker branches, or even helping to construct a makeshift shelter if you're planning an extended stay, a survival knife answers the call. It's a multifaceted instrument, as adaptable as the Green Witch wielding it, making it an indispensable part of your foraging excursions.

So, as you shoulder your foraging bag and step into the wild, make sure to carry your survival knife. It's more than just a tool; it's a testament to your commitment to be prepared, adaptable, and respectful towards the natural world you're interacting with. And that, in essence, is the heart of a Green Witch's foraging ethos.

Gloves: The Protective Veil Between You and the Wilderness
As you plunge your hands into the verdant expanse of nature's undergrowth to extract medicinal herbs, the need for protective gloves becomes abundantly clear. The world of wild flora is rich and diverse, but alongside its myriad benefits, it holds potential hazards, too. Thorny branches, abrasive foliage, and plants like poison ivy that can trigger an allergic response are all part of the experience. The essence of a Green Witch is about mindful interaction with nature, and gloves serve as your protective veil in this relationship.

Imagine you're deep into your foraging expedition, eyes alight with the beauty of the natural world around you. Suddenly, your fingers brush against the concealed thorns of a bramble or the glossy leaves of a poison ivy. Without gloves, you risk painful pricks, scratches, or a bothersome rash. Protective gloves eliminate this risk, allowing you to delve into the thickest of undergrowth with confidence and safety.

It's not just about protection, though. Wearing gloves also enhances your ability to interact with the various textures of the wilderness, to feel the rough bark of a tree or the smooth surface of a leaf without concern. They facilitate a seamless connection with nature, allowing you to touch, feel, and explore with your hands with added security.

Complementing your gloves with long sleeves is another wise choice, ensuring an additional layer of protection for your arms when you delve into dense foliage or reach into the depths of tall, leafy plants. Dressing for foraging should be akin to preparing for yard work; gear up, respect the potential challenges of nature, and make safety a priority.

Remember, donning a pair of gloves is more than a defensive measure. It signifies your intent to respect and protect both yourself and the natural world you're engaging with. Because, as a Green Witch, your duty is to foster a relationship with nature that is steeped in respect, mindfulness, and reciprocity - and gloves play a pivotal role in facilitating this relationship.

Small Magnifying Glass: An Insightful Lens Into Nature's Minutiae
Becoming an effective Green Witch necessitates a keen eye for detail. However, some elements of the wild are so minuscule, they pose a challenge to the naked eye. That's where a small magnifying glass steps into the picture, transforming your foraging excursions into detailed explorations of nature's minutiae.

As you wander through the wilderness, you'll encounter plants with tiny, intricate features—minute flowers, delicate seed pods, or subtly patterned leaves—whose identities are crucial to your craft. Here, your small magnifying glass emerges as a vital tool. By magnifying these minuscule features, it offers you a chance to study and appreciate the intricate beauty that often goes unnoticed.

But the magnifying glass isn't just a tool for curiosity; it's an aid for accuracy. With it, you can accurately identify different plant species, deciphering similar-looking ones that might otherwise cause confusion. It bridges the gap between visual ambiguity and clear identification, ensuring you harvest the right plants and herbs for your potions, infusions, or tinctures.

Now, let's consider a common concern for many of us—diminishing eyesight. As we age, our visual acuity naturally declines, making it harder to perceive small details. If you're in the same boat, the magnifying glass doubles up as a handy assistant. It amplifies nature's intricate details, making them easy to spot and discern even if your eyesight isn't as sharp as it used to be.

So, as a foraging Green Witch, remember to pack a small magnifying glass in your toolkit. It's compact and light, but its impact on your foraging pursuits is immense. This simple lens will become your window to the intricate details of the plant world, empowering you to fully appreciate and accurately identify the botanical wonders that surround you.

5-Gallon Bucket: The Green Witch's Toting Essential

The role of a 5-gallon bucket in the foraging journey cannot be overstated. This seemingly simple object embodies profound functionality, offering a steadfast and reliable method to carry your multitude of foraging tools. It is more than just a container; it is a crucial accessory that facilitates your exploration of the wild.

In the heart of nature, you might encounter medicinal trees laden with branches or encounter areas brimming with robust tubers. Gathering these valuable treasures calls for a dependable companion, and the 5-gallon bucket steps in to fulfill that role. Its sturdy structure and ample capacity allow you to easily pile up your collections and transport them without inconvenience. The bucket's pragmatic design, with its robust handle and spacious interior, enables you to navigate through the wilderness with ease, keeping your focus on the task of foraging.

Baskets: The Gentle Carriers for Delicate Forage

When it comes to carrying more delicate foraging finds such as tender plants, berries, and flowers, foraging baskets come into play. These charming receptacles, available in an array of shapes and sizes, are specifically designed for the gentler side of foraging.

Unlike the solid, unyielding walls of a 5-gallon bucket, baskets offer a softer cradle. Their woven structure provides a bit of give, carefully holding your precious harvest without crushing their delicate forms. This quality is essential when dealing with fragile wild edibles or medicinal plants that need to be kept in their natural state as much as possible.

The beauty of a foraging basket is not only in its practicality but also in the touch of tradition it adds to your foraging practice. Whether you're lightly filling it with wildflowers from a sun-drenched meadow or carefully piling it with ripe berries from a forest's edge, the basket serves as a gentle reminder of the ancient roots of foraging.

Therefore, having both a sturdy 5-gallon bucket and a gentle foraging basket in your toolkit gives you the flexibility and preparedness to handle the varied treasures you'll encounter on your wild harvesting adventures.

Harvesting with Respect: Nurturing a Sustainable Connection with Nature

As foragers of the green witch tradition, we must always remember: the world is not our personal garden. We are stepping into nature's domain, engaging with the wild, and taking what we need. But unlike a backyard garden where you dictate the terms, in nature, we are merely guests.

The distinction between harvesting from our personal gardens and foraging from the wild is crucial. When we plant, nourish, and tend to a garden, we rightfully claim its yield. However, the bounty of nature is not solely ours. The wild provides for countless creatures, and as responsible foragers, we owe it to all life forms to tread lightly, leaving the smallest footprint possible.

The practice of foraging is not a one-way transaction; it's a delicate balance, a dance of give and take. By over-harvesting or exploiting wild resources, we disrupt that balance, compromising the survival of these life-sustaining ecosystems.

Therefore, responsible foraging is an essential tenet of our journey. It commences with understanding the plants you intend to harvest. Only by recognizing a plant's needs and life cycle can you ensure its continuous survival and propagation, preserving the natural wealth for future generations and the myriad other creatures that rely on it.

For example, when you encounter a patch of wild plants, a responsible forager leaves at least 25% of the population untouched. This measure, while seeming small, helps ensure the plant's survival and propagation. As a result, you secure a lasting connection with that spot, promising more fruitful harvests in the years to come.

This principle can be more complex when it comes to harvesting roots and tubers. Since these parts are vital to the plant's life, merely sparing a fraction of the rootstock won't ensure the plant's survival. In such cases, it's crucial to consider the broader ecosystem. If

you're harvesting sassafras roots, for example, look around to ensure a healthy stand of saplings and mature trees remain. Leaving a quarter of these unharvested gives them a chance to propagate and replenish the population.

Responsible foraging also carries a silver lining: roots often hold potent healing properties, and typically, a small quantity suffices for our needs.

Embrace your role as a forager of wild medicine with humility and responsibility. We are intertwined with the natural world, and as stewards of the land, we owe it to the planet and its inhabitants to harvest with care and respect. Remember, foraging is a privilege, not a right. Cherish it and use it wisely.

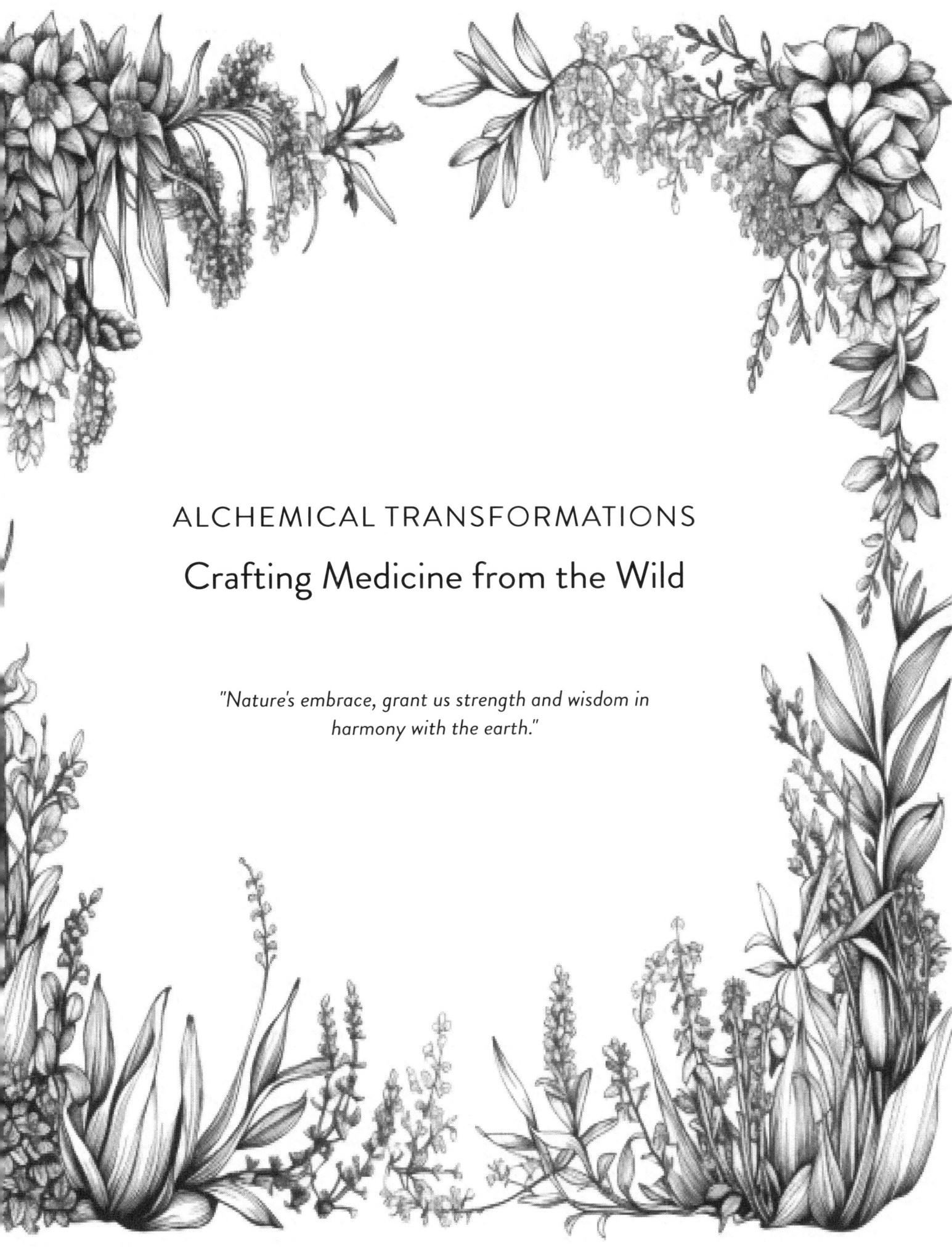

ALCHEMICAL TRANSFORMATIONS

Crafting Medicine from the Wild

"Nature's embrace, grant us strength and wisdom in harmony with the earth."

From recognizing the whispers of nature to respectfully harvesting her generous offerings, our journey as Green Witches is a dance with the Earth. It spirals towards the grand finale - the transformation of these bountiful elements into potent plant medicine. This act of alchemical transmutation, of turning raw, wild flora into healing potions, is where we truly embody our craft.

These techniques are the bedrock upon which we build our botanical pharmacy. Each has a unique rhythm, a distinctive story to tell, and a specific gift to bestow. Some methods, like crafting salves, speak to the skin and the body's surface, providing healing in the physical realm. Meanwhile, others, like hot infusions, sing a song of inner wellness, delivering their potent whispers to the innermost corners of our being.

Upon gathering your green allies from the wild, the stage is set for their metamorphosis. The act of processing is a sacred rite, a delicate dance that unlocks the secret healing songs within the plants, allowing them to become usable, effective treatments.

Now, let us unfurl the scroll of botanical knowledge. The following sections will delve into the magical and practical arts of plant processing, each a unique pathway to healing. As we traverse these paths together, you will be laying the foundation of your craft, evolving into a skilled weaver of wild medicine.

Crafting Poultices from the Earth's Bounty

A poultice, dear reader, is a salve of the earth, a whisper of nature's inherent healing powers. It's a bundle of magic that cradles the body, eases its pains, reduces inflammation, and ushers in an era of rest and recovery. Born from fresh plant material, a poultice is a testament to the immediacy and potency of Mother Earth's offerings.

Perchance, you've been graced by the green lady of the common plantain. A humble guest in most gardens, her emerald veined leaves hold an ageless wisdom of healing. She humbly offers her aid, surrendering her leaves to be chewed and transformed into a poultice. Applied directly to a wound, plantain poultice becomes an instant healer, purifying and nursing the wound, even when other remedies are out of reach.

A poultice must be shielded, protected like a delicate secret whispered into the wind. Once lovingly spread over the affected area, it must be swaddled, be it with bandages, a clean cloth, or even a leaf large enough to shelter its healing power. It forms a bridge between the suffering body and the healing earth, offering solace in a time of immediate need.

A poultice is a fleeting song of healing, echoing in the stillness, and vanishing as swiftly as it comes. It demands immediate creation and use, discouraging storage. The strength of a poultice lies in its freshness, in the instantaneous communion between the living plant and the body seeking relief.

In the wild, where gears and tools may be scarce, a poultice shines as a beacon of immediate healing. It is the first aid of the forest, a testament to the symbiotic bond between us witches and the living, breathing earth.

Top of Form

The Art of Creating Tinctures

In the grand alchemical symphony of the universe, the creation of tinctures holds a unique place. It's a dance, a graceful interplay between potent plant essences and the catalytic properties of alcohol. Like a long, silent waltz, the process of making a tincture requires time, patience, and a deep understanding of the rhythm of nature.

A tincture isn't a remedy birthed in the immediacy of need, like a poultice. It's a plan, a seed sown today to reap the benefits weeks, even a month, later. It's about listening to the silent whispers of the plant world, understanding the delicate leaves' willingness to yield their essence within a week, while the resilient bark may guard its secrets for a month.

While some may sing praises to the robust spirits of rum, brandy, or whiskey, I find my rhythm in the quiet company of vodka. It is the silent partner in this dance, bringing no color, odor, or flavor of its own, but magnifying the plant's melody in its purity. Or perhaps, if fortune favors you with moonshine, the dance becomes even more intoxicating.

Alcohol, in this dance, is the catalyst. Its skill at coaxing out the spirits, essences, and resins of plants is unparalleled. It has a particular fondness for the silent stories held within the woody bark and fibrous roots, drawing them out into a potent potion of healing.

The waltz begins with 7 ounces of chopped leaves, roots, or bark, and a liter of alcohol, meeting in the quiet sanctuary of a glass container. I prefer a humble mason jar for this. A gentle stir, a secure lid, and the silent dance begins, lasting anywhere between a week to a month.

The final act of this dance sees the tincture settling in its final abode, a brown glass jar or bottle. An eyedropper is ideal for serving this potion of wellness, a humble reminder of the time and patience that went into its creation. And thus, the dance concludes, leaving behind a precious tincture, a testament to the harmony between nature and us witches.

Crafting Infused Oils

Let us turn our gaze towards the quiet magic of infused oils. These gentle brews often go overlooked in their simplicity, yet they carry within them the potent whispers of nature's wisdom.

Infused oils are like bottling the soul of a plant. This process allows us to harness the strength of a medicinal herb, its very essence seeping into the oil. Creating these potent potions is a straightforward affair, guided by the humble ratio of one part herb to five parts oil. As witches, we only engage in dances with the purest partners, and so for your oils, choose only the highest quality, cold-pressed oils. The purity of your ingredients will guide the effectiveness of your infused oils.

Crafting Salves

Salves, my dear, are the comforting hugs of wild medicine. At their core, you'll find a harmonious union of beeswax and carrier oil. These two elements meld together, creating a nurturing base that welcomes the medicinal plant.

Here's a simple incantation to create your salve:

- One cup of a carrier oil - olive oil or grapeseed oil are good partners
- Half a cup of your chosen medicinal plant, chopped or crushed
- Four tablespoons of beeswax

In this magical fusion, the consistency of your salve is crucial. Test it by drawing a spoonful of the mixture and allowing it to cool. It should retain a creamy texture, not hardening into a solid mass. Remember, this dance of creation is all about balance. If your salve feels too hard, whisper in a little more oil. If it's too loose, invite more beeswax to join the mix.

In crafting these infused oils and salves, we're capturing whispers of nature's wisdom. They're not just medicines but stories, tales of the earth's abundance and generosity that we can keep close to our hearts. They're gentle reminders that even the simplest of creations can carry within them the profoundest healing.

Top of Form

Hot Infusion

Let me guide you now to the world of infusions, where the fire of the boiling cauldron and the gentle heat of the sun come to play. Infusions are akin to brewing magical teas, where the medicinal whispers of the plants imbue the water, creating a simple yet potent brew.

Hot infusions tap into the fiery energy of boiling water. This process involves the simmering dance of heated water and plant material. Bring your water to a boil and gently pour it over the plant parts, allowing them to steep in the water's embrace for 5 to 15 minutes. Strain the remnants of the plant and sip your steaming medicine, a potion brewed with intention. A general guide would be 2 cups of boiling water introduced to 2 ounces of fresh plant material.

Cold Infusion

Now, let's turn our gaze from the vigorous dance of the boiling cauldron to the serene ballet of sun and water. Cold infusions, much like sun tea, engage the gentle warmth of the sun. Rather than immersing the plant material in hot water, we opt for cool, clear water placed in a glass jar. Ideally, choose a jar with a lid to keep the magic contained. Place your jar under the sun's watchful gaze and let it rest for a few hours. Allow the sunlight to weave its warmth into your infusion, encouraging the plant's essence to meld with the water.

Cold infusions are perfect for more delicate medicines, particularly those of a leafy nature. The boiling water of a hot infusion can sometimes be too fierce for such tender plant materials. The sunlight's gentle warmth offers a softer way to draw out their medicinal properties.

Whether you choose to walk with the fire or dance with the sun, infusions are a beautiful testament to the power of simplicity. They remind us that the union of water and plant material, whether guided by heat or sun, can yield potent medicines, filled with nature's wisdom.

Decoctions

Decoctions blend the artistry of infusions with an added element of heat, creating a symphony of simmering magic. Like a chef preparing a luscious stock or a vibrant sauce, you will be called to bring the herbs to life through the alchemy of heat and water.

Unlike an infusion, where the herbs meet already-boiled water, a decoction invites the herbs to dance in the water as it transitions from cool to boiling. The mixture is then allowed to simmer for about 20 minutes, the heat coaxing out the medicinal properties of the herbs, infusing the water with their essence.

Once the simmering serenade ends, allow the decoction to cool to room temperature, letting the plant matter and water continue their intimate exchange. Then, strain the liquid, capturing the concentrated herbal brew.

Here is a simple guide for your first decoction: • 1 Cup of Water • 2-4 Tablespoons of Fresh Herbs

Once ready, savor your decoction, drinking a cup every 1-2 hours. This slow and steady consumption allows your body to truly absorb the healing properties of the herbs, promoting wellbeing from within.

Decoctions remind us of the deep magic that arises from time, patience, and gentle heat. In the simmering dance of herbs and water, we find a potent brew imbued with the whispers of the plant world, a symphony of simmering magic ready to nurture our bodies and souls.

Fomentations: Healing Cloths Bathed in Nature's Brew

Fomentations carry the healing whispers of the plants directly to the skin's surface. While not a medicine in the traditional sense, these plant-infused compresses hold a deep power to heal and soothe. They are the gentle caresses of the green witch, tending to her own and her community with wisdom drawn from the Earth.

Imagine a cloth bathed in a healing decoction or hot infusion, soaking up the herbal essences like a sponge absorbs water. This cloth, now imbued with the plant's medicinal properties, is gently laid upon the body's surface, like a warm, healing hand.

The fomentation can be applied to bruises, rashes, or aches, even gently laid over closed eyes to soothe headaches. The warm cloth clings to the skin, the healing properties seeping into the affected area. And it is not just the plants that are at work here. The heat, too, plays its part, softening and soothing, helping to ease discomfort and promote healing.

Here's how you create this magical tool:

1. Dip a clean, soft cloth into your decoction or hot infusion. Let it drink in the brew, soaking up the healing wisdom of the plants.

2. Wring out the excess liquid but leave the cloth comfortably damp.

3. Apply this warm, medicinal cloth to the affected area, letting it rest there as long as it stays warm.

Remember, dear green witch, that you weave together the power of the natural world with the wisdom of your heart when you use these tools. Fomentations are more than warm compresses. They are tangible expressions of your caring and your connection with the Earth, bringing comfort and healing in times of need.

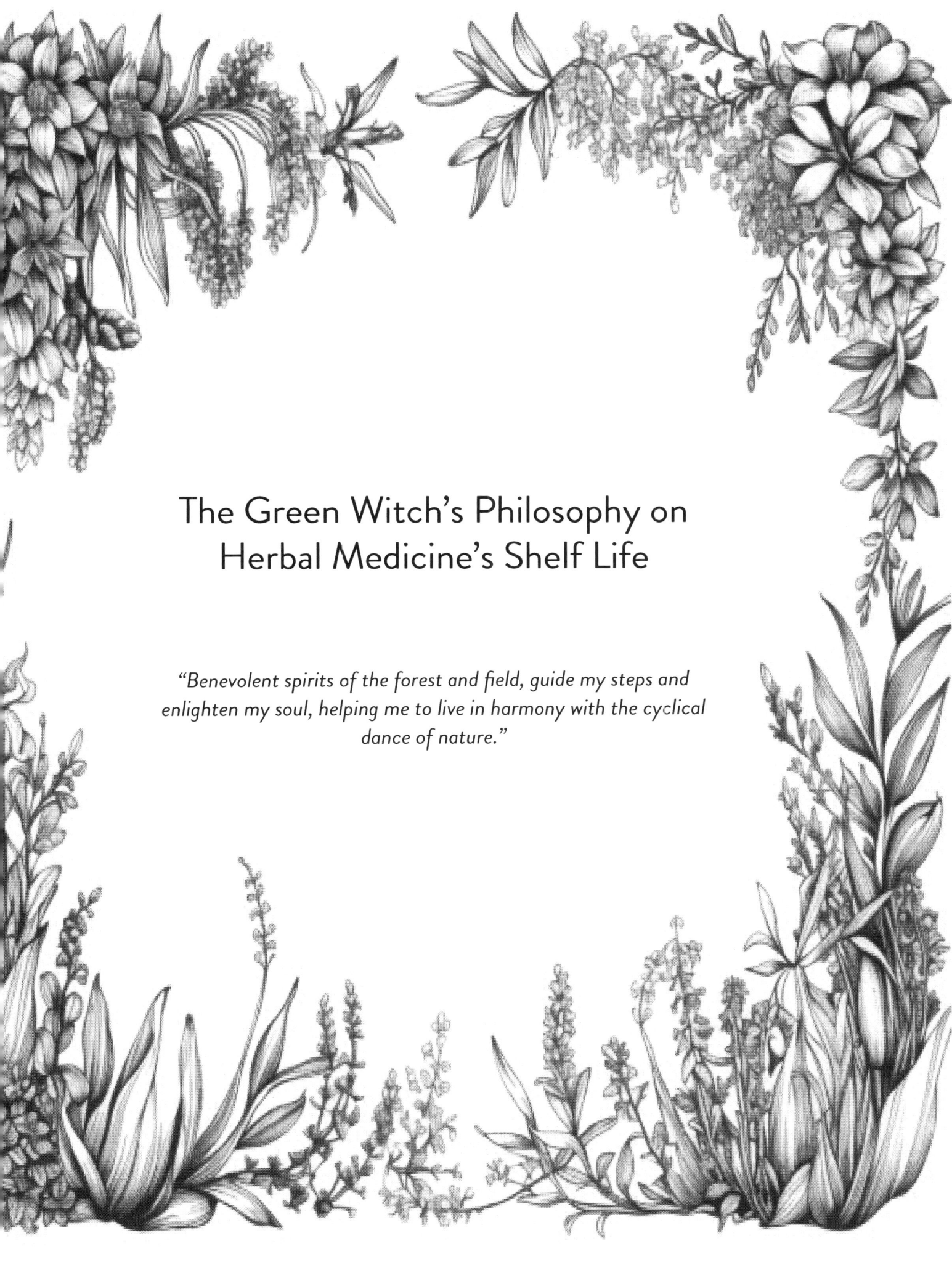

The Green Witch's Philosophy on Herbal Medicine's Shelf Life

"Benevolent spirits of the forest and field, guide my steps and enlighten my soul, helping me to live in harmony with the cyclical dance of nature."

Let us pause to ponder the question of the longevity of our herbal allies. Yes, it is a truth universally recognized in the herbal community that tinctures and other alcohol-based preparations can last for many years. But should they? Is the question of whether they can outlive their usefulness more important than whether they should?

As a green witch, my craft is intimately connected with the cycles of nature. And nature, dear friend, is not static. It is ever-changing, ever-renewing. So why should my medicine be any different? Why should I hold on to a tincture for five years when the plant it came from lives and dies with the changing seasons?

When I prepare medicine for my family and community, it is an offering of love and care. I gather plants in their prime, full of vitality, and I prepare my medicine with reverence and mindfulness. The resulting brew is not merely a collection of plant compounds; it is the very essence of the plant, captured in a moment of its life cycle.

After a day, even the freshest of herbs begin to lose their vitality. Exposed to the air, their vibrant colors fade, their aromas dissipate, and their therapeutic properties diminish. After a year, how much of their essence can remain in a jar?

For me, the rhythm of herbal medicine preparation is seasonal. Each year, as the plants grow, bloom, and recede, I make my medicines. And each year, as the new growth appears, I replace the old with the new. This is not a rule dictated by any book or authority; it is my personal rhythm, my dance with the plants and the seasons.

There are, of course, exceptions. Salves, for instance, with their rich base of oils and beeswax, can last for more than a year without losing their potency. And the harder parts of the plants - the roots and barks - take longer to release their essence, so a root or bark tincture might well retain its potency for longer than a year.

This rhythm may not suit everyone, but for me, it is a vital part of my green witch path. It keeps me connected to the natural cycles, reminds me of the impermanence and preciousness of life, and ensures that the medicine I offer is as fresh, vibrant, and potent as it can be.

Wild Herb Habitats – A Green Witch's Travelogue

My dear apprentices, welcome to the Green Witch's Travelogue, a wondrous journey through the diverse habitats of our beloved Mother Earth. As we embark on this journey, remember, recognizing the myriad environments of our world is a vital step in understanding the myriad ways she supports us with her abundant medicinal treasures.

Every plant and herb we seek has a favorite place, a chosen habitat where it thrives best. To truly know a plant, we must know its home. That knowledge is as crucial as understanding the hue of its petals or the pattern of its leaves.

Picture this: You spend a day wandering in the eastern woodlands, your heart yearning for a particular herb, only to discover that your desired companion thrives in the craggy heights of mountainous regions. What a dance you've had, only to realize you were swaying to the wrong tune!

Or imagine seeking a magical medicine that prefers the whispering company of pine forests. Would you be looking amongst the golden waves of prairies or the salty air of coastal regions? Of course not! The symphony of pine needles beneath your boots would guide your steps.

Understanding habitat, dear ones, is like holding a magical map to the herbal kingdom. It narrows your search, focuses your energy, and enriches your connection with the world around you. It's not merely another way to identify plants—it's a way to connect deeply with the vibrant web of life in which we all partake.

So, take your travelogue, my dear green witches, and let the knowledge of habitats guide your steps, enrich your journey, and deepen your bond with Mother Earth. After all, in our dance with her, every step, every habitat, every plant matters. The whole Earth is our home, and every corner of it has wisdom to share with us, if only we take the time to listen and learn.

Wetlands: A Mirrored Realm of Medicinal Treasures

Wetlands are more prevalent than one might think. As sanctuaries for diverse ecosystems, they're swiftly gaining protected status, which can make foraging in them a bit tricky. But, dear witches, wherever you find bodies of water—creeks, lakes, rivers—you'll likely find wetlands nearby. These aquatic abodes are teeming with medicinal gifts. Near these water sources, you'll find the healing white willow and the mighty black walnut. So don your best boots and explore these vibrant marshlands; the rewards are worth the wet feet!

Coastal: Where Land Meets Sea, Medicine Grows

Coastal regions, where the land kisses the sea, are wonderful places to seek wild medicinal plants. The loamy soil, enriched by the ebb and flow of the tides, is fertile ground for many kinds of plants. While the number of medicinal plants may not be as high as in other habitats, don't overlook these sea-kissed lands; they have their own unique offerings.

Deciduous Forests: The Changing Canvas of Healing

Deciduous forests, the artists of the plant world, paint vibrant pictures with their leaves that fall in winter. These woodlands are home to a treasure trove of medicinal trees—dogwood, walnut, willow, cherry, and more. As you wander amongst these color-changing trees, look for the gifts they scatter with each passing season.

Old Stands: Ancient Wisdom in Bark and Leaf

The evergreen forests, eternally draped in green, host healing companions such as the mighty pine. These forests, dominated by needle-bearing trees, have unique characteristics that can be tapped for wild medicine making. Step into their timeless embrace, and you might just discover the secrets they keep all year round.

Evergreen Forests: The Enduring Green Healers

The evergreen forests, eternally draped in green, host healing companions such as the mighty pine. These forests, dominated by needle-bearing trees, have unique characteristics that can be tapped for wild medicine making. Step into their timeless embrace, and you might just discover the secrets they keep all year round.

Prairies and Fields: The Unfettered Gardens of Mother Earth

Prairies and fields, those open expanses of swaying grasses and wildflowers, are dominated by medicinal flowers and roots. Unhindered by tree canopies, these habitats allow their floral inhabitants to bathe freely in sunlight. They may seem simple, but do not underestimate their bounty.

Highlands: The Elevated Gardens of the Sky

In many areas, you'll find highland habitats where the land begins to rise into hilly regions or plateaus. These higher elevations, with their crisp air and panoramic views, are home to many unique species found nowhere else. Some medicinal herbs prefer these lofty habitats, their virtues enhanced by the highland air.

Mountains: The Rocky Citadels of Green Wisdom
Mountainous regions offer diverse opportunities for the forager. Lower elevations can host a range of medicinal plants and trees, while higher, rocky, evergreen-dominated areas provide their own unique gifts. Don't let the steep slopes deter you; the mountains have their own unique way of nurturing life.

Spring's Medicinals
REGISTER OF PLANTS, HERBS, AND THEIR HEALING GIFTS

Birch Tree (Pain and Fever)

Clover, red (Expectorant Women's Health)

Dandelion (Stimulates Digestion)

Garlic (Infection)

Hyssop (Digestion)

Jewelweed (Poison Ivy Treatment)

Mullein (Respiratory)

Queen Annes Lace

Staghorn Sumac (High Vitamin C)

Veronica (Respiratory)

Violets (Skin Irritation and Inflammation)

Summer's Medicinals
REGISTER OF PLANTS, HERBS,
AND THEIR HEALING GIFTS

Angelica (Chest and Lung Cough)

Bee Balm (External, Skin Scrapes and Stings)

Borage (Digestive System)

Burdock (Digestive System)

Calendula (Internal Inflammation)

Cayenne (Inflammation)

Cherry (Lungs Cough)

Comfrey (Skin Issues)

Cornflower (Inflammation, Skin)

Echinacea (Cold and Immune System)

Elderberry (Cold and Immune)

Feverfew (Fever)

Ginger (Infection Inflammation)

Ginseng (Symptoms)

Goldenseal (Respiratory)

Horse Chestnut (Skin care and varicose veins)

Jasmine (Anxiety)

Lavender (Wound Healing Hair Loss)

Lemon Balm (Anxiety)

Maple Tree (Sedative Tea)

Mullein (Respiratory)

Milk Thistle (Promotes Appetite Aids in Digestion)

Mint (Headaches Digestion)

Oregano (Antibacterial)

Passionflower (Sedative and Sleep Aid)

Stinging Nettle (Immune System, Muscle and Joint Pain)

Willow (Pain Fever)

Yarrow (Bleeding)

Fall's Medicinals
REGISTER OF PLANTS, HERBS, AND THEIR HEALING GIFTS

Ash (Rheumatism, Jaundice, Gout)

Black Walnut (Bleeding, Constipation)

Feverfew (Fever)

Ginger (Infection Inflammation)

Ginseng (Symptoms)

Goldenseal (Respiratory)

Hawthorne (Heart Treatment Blood Pressure)

Hazelnut (Hazelnut Oil Protects Skin from Sun and Skin Issues)

Milk Thistle (Promotes Appetite Aids in Digestion)

Oregano (Antibacterial)

Passionflower (Sedative and Sleep Aid)

Pine Tree (Vitamin C Immunity)

Rose (Cooling, Boosting, Immunity)

Sage (Respiratory Mouth and Gum)

Stinging Nettle (Immune System, Muscle and Joint Pain)

Watercress (Congestion Bronchitis)

Willow (Pain Fever)

Winter's Medicinals
REGISTER OF PLANTS, HERBS,
AND THEIR HEALING GIFTS

Arnica (Skin Conditions)

Balsam Poplar (Skin Conditions Pain Relief)

Black Walnut (Bleeding, Constipation)

Evening Primrose (Arthritis Skin Inflammation)

Rosemary (Overall Health)

St John's Wort (Depression, Sleep Aid)

Sea Buckthorn (Respiratory Vitamin C)

Skullcap (Sedative)

Slippery Elm (Sore Throat)

Thyme (Antibacterial)

Watercress (Congestion Bronchitis)

Witch Hazel (External Skin Issues)

Wild Lettuce (Pain Respiratory Anxiety)

Willow (Pain Fever)

Wintergreen (Fever Pain Inflammation)

Alphabetical List of the
Medicinal Plants and Herbs

Angelica (Angelica archangelica)

Plant Name: Angelica

Lore: In ancient Europe, amidst the devastation of the plague, legend has it that an angel appeared to a monk, revealing the plant that could combat the disease. Due to its medicinal prowess and this legend, it was named Angelica.

What Does it Treat? Angelica has been traditionally used to treat chest and lung conditions, as well as rheumatism. Chewing the roots may promote urination.

Habitat & Region: Angelica thrives in Deciduous Woodlands and Wetlands.

Identification: The distinguishing feature of Angelica is its globe-shaped clusters of flowers. Each plant has several of these globe clusters perched atop long stems.

- **Flowers:** The umbrella-like, clustered flowers are predominantly white but can sometimes exhibit a pinkish hue.
- **Leaves:** Bearing a dagger-like silhouette, the leaves are symmetrical and taper to a point. Their resemblance to poison hemlock leaves necessitates caution during identification.

Medicinal Parts: The stalks, leaves, flowers, and fruits of the Angelica plant are harnessed for medicinal purposes.

How to Harvest: Despite its delicate nature, Angelica can be harvested with care.

Making Medicine: For an Angelica Tea or Hot Infusion, combine 1 teaspoon of dried root with 1 cup of boiling water. Allow the mixture to steep for 10-20 minutes.

Dosage: Recommended consumption is 2-3 times per day.

WARNINGS: Angelica bears a striking resemblance to the deadly poison hemlock. Their shared characteristics, including leaves and flower clusters, can lead to fatal misidentifications. Consuming poison hemlock is lethal. To reduce risks, it is advised to use the garden variety of Angelica for medicinal purposes. While it's rarer, it provides peace of mind with easier identification. Acquaint yourself thoroughly with Angelica's characteristics before wild harvesting to avoid dangerous mistakes.

Garden variety Angelica is preferred for making medicine and would give you less to worry about as far as identification. It is rare but I think this would be a better solution until you get good at identifying this plant.

Arnica (Arnica montana)

Plant Name: Arnica

Plant Type: Perennial Ground Plant

Lore: Legend has it that sprinkling arnica around one's property not only provides protection but also bestows fertility upon the garden.

What Does it Treat: Arnica is renowned for its effectiveness in treating skin issues such as rashes, boils, and acne. Additionally, it is a potent remedy for swelling.

Habitat & Region: Arnica thrives exclusively in the Northwest Uplands of North America.

Identification: Arnica undergoes a lifecycle reminiscent of the dandelion. It bears a resemblance to a miniature sunflower and emerges from a tall stalk, with rosette-shaped leaves at the base.

- **Flowers:** Radiant yellow with a central yellow hub, the flower closely mirrors the appearance of a small sunflower.
- **Leaves:** The rosette leaves, located at the base of the long stem, are also characterized by the presence of minute hairs.

Medicinal Parts: The flowers of Arnica are the most potent and are ideal for harvesting.

How to Harvest: Arnica, being delicate, can be effortlessly uprooted from the ground. Alternatively, the flowers can be carefully snipped or plucked.

Making Medicine:
Arnica Infused Oil: Begin by placing Arnica flowers in a mason jar, ensuring they are submerged in oil. Opt for a high-quality carrier oil to cover the flowers. While olive oil is a viable option, a neutral oil like grapeseed is often recommended. Direct sunlight can degrade olive oil, making it less ideal for this infusion. Position your jar in a sunlit window, allowing it to steep for several weeks. Once infused, strain to separate the flowers, reserving the golden-hued oil. Ensure it's stored in a cool, dark location.

Arnica Salve

- Start with the Arnica infused oil

- Follow our provided salve recipe.

- While the salve is still warm, decant it into a tin. Like the oil, store the salve in a cool, shaded spot.

Dosage: Gently apply to the affected skin area as required.

WARNINGS: It's imperative to note that Arnica resembles various other plants. Dedicate time to familiarize yourself with Arnica, ensuring you can confidently identify it to avoid potential mix-ups with other plants.

Ash Trees (Fraxinus sp.)

Plant Name: Ash Tree

Plant Type: Ash

Lore: The ash tree holds a revered position in Norse Mythology. Yggdrasill, known as the World Tree, is identified as an ash tree. Moreover, the spears wielded by the Norse gods Odin and Thor were believed to have been crafted from ash wood.

What Does it Treat: Historically, remedies derived from the ash tree have been used to address conditions like rheumatism, jaundice, and gout.

Habitat & Region: Ash trees predominantly grow in Deciduous Forests.

Identification: Ash trees possess a distinctive light grey bark.

- **Flowers:** Initially, the ash tree displays black flower buds. These later transform into white and purple hues.
- **Leaves:** Each branch of the ash tree carries 4-8 opposite lance-shaped leaves.
- **Keys:** Commonly referred to as "keys", the fruit of the ash tree comprises a seed encased within a wing-like structure..

Medicinal Parts: Primarily, the leaves of the Ash Tree are used for medicinal purposes.

How to Harvest: To harvest ash tree leaves for medicinal uses, trim the branches, ensuring to hang them to dry, as dried leaves are preferred for making tea.

Making Medicine: To prepare Ash Leaf Tea, mix 2 tablespoons of dried ash leaves with 1 cup of boiling water. Allow the mixture to steep for about 10 minutes.

Dosage: For best results, consume the ash tree tea 2-3 times daily.

WARNINGS: Ensure accurate identification of the ash tree, as there are other trees with similar features.

It's essential to be cautious about the quantity of ash tree preparations consumed. Overconsumption might lead to adverse effects.

Always consult with a knowledgeable herbalist or healthcare provider before using ash leaves medicinally, especially for individuals with underlying health conditions or those taking other medications.

Balsam Poplar (Populus balsamifera)

Plant Name: Balsam Poplar

Plant Type: Deciduous Tree

Lore: The Balsam Poplar stands as the northernmost American hardwood tree.

What Does it Treat: Balsam Poplar has various medicinal components that aid in treating skin conditions, rashes, and aiding wound healing. Additionally, it's known for its pain-relieving properties.

Habitat & Region: This tree is primarily found in deciduous forests situated alongside streams and wetlands.

Identification Often referred to as the black cottonwood, the Balsam Poplar is characterized by its leathery arrowhead-shaped leaves and grey bark. A distinguishing feature is its towering stature, with the tree often reaching heights between 100 and 165 feet.

- **Flowers:** Instead of traditional flowers, the Balsam Poplar presents small red catkins.
- **Leaves:** Notable for their substantial size, these leaves are thick, leathery, and mimic a broad arrowhead shape with rounded tips.
- **Bark:** The tree's grey bark is striated, which is a common feature among trees of its kind.

Medicinal Parts: The tree's leaf buds are enveloped in a resin, which is typically separated through boiling and then dissolved in alcohol. These buds are also brewed to make tea. The inner bark, being mucilaginous, can be dried and powdered for medicinal use.

How to Harvest: For medicinal purposes, young leaf buds should be gently plucked or snipped from the tree.

Making Medicine: To craft a Balsam oil, carry a pint-sized glass jar during your harvest and collect resinous leaf buds of the Balsam Poplar until it's ¾ full. Once home, top the jar with a carrier oil such as grapeseed or olive oil. Immerse this jar in a small saucepot filled with water. Initiate the extraction by warming the water over low heat for about 4-6 hours. Upon completion, strain the mixture to obtain the pure balsam oil.

To create a Balsam salve, combine approximately ¼ cup of beeswax for every cup of balsam oil. Gently warm the mixture, ensuring thorough amalgamation, and then decant into a wide-mouth container.

Dosage: Apply the salve to the affected area as and when required.

WARNINGS: Always ensure proper identification of the Balsam Poplar as there are several trees with similar characteristics. Before topical application or consumption, it's advisable to conduct a patch test or consult a healthcare practitioner, especially for individuals with sensitivities or allergies. While the Balsam Poplar is revered for its medicinal properties, excessive use or ingestion could lead to adverse effects.

Barberry (Berberis sp.)

Plant Name: Barberry

Plant Type: Evergreen Deciduous Shrub

Lore: The medicinal prowess of this shrub primarily stems from its active compound, berberine.

What Does it Treat: Barberry is especially adept at treating infections and inflammations across various systems in the body, including the urinary, digestive, and respiratory systems. The compound berberine found in barberry is a potent antibacterial, antiprotozoal, and antifungal agent.

Habitat & Region: Barberry naturally thrives at forest edges and can often be spotted amidst roadside brambles.

Identification: A fully-grown barberry shrub can stretch up to 9 feet in height. Its stems are easily identifiable thanks to the long, sharp thorns they bear.

- **Flowers:** The shrub exhibits clusters of flowers that predominantly carry a yellow hue with slight red undertones.
- **Leaves:** Barberry leaves are oval in shape with toothed edges. Though thin, they have a slightly scrubby texture.
- **Fruits:** The red berries that emerge from the drooping yellow flower clusters are notably rich in Vitamin C.

Medicinal Parts: The berries are a powerhouse of Vitamin C, and the root bark is often harnessed to concoct a potent tincture.

How to Harvest: A tool like the Hori hori knife is exceptionally useful when attempting to extract the roots.

Making Medicine: To make a Barberry Root Bark tincture, adhere to a 1:10 ratio with 50% alcohol.

Dosage: Given the tincture's strength, it's advised to limit the dosage to no more than 12ml per day.

WARNINGS: Excessive consumption of barberry, especially in tincture form, might lead to adverse effects. It's essential to adhere to recommended dosages and always consult with a healthcare professional before use.

Properly identify barberry before harvesting, as there are other plants with similar appearances that may not be safe for consumption or medicinal use.

Pregnant or breastfeeding women should avoid using barberry, as berberine can cross the placenta and might cause harm. It may also be transferred to infants through breast milk.

Bee Balm (Monarda sp.)

Plant Name: Bee Balm

Plant Type: Rhizomatous perennial herb

Lore: Commonly known as wild bergamot, bee balm is a primary flavoring agent in the iconic Earl Grey tea.

What Does it Treat: Bee balm boasts antimicrobial properties and exudes a soothing effect. When applied externally, it effectively addresses issues like minor wounds, insect stings, and skin rashes.

Habitat & Region: This plant finds its natural home in prairies, thickets, and woodland edges that receive ample sunlight.

Identification: Bee balm, or wild bergamot, has the potential to grow up to three feet in height. Its lavender-hued flowers are irresistible to bees and other pollinators, making it a vibrant hub of activity.

- **Flowers:** The flowers of the bee balm are uniquely tubular and resemble exploding lavender fireworks crowning the plant.
- **Leaves:** These are spear-shaped with serrated edges, providing a distinct contrast to the vibrant flowers.

How to Harvest: The leaves and flowers of the bee balm are both edible and beneficial for medicinal use. Harvesting can be done manually or with the aid of shears.

Making Medicine: Bee Balm Hot Infusion and Tea: Combine 1 tablespoon of bee balm flowers with 1 cup of boiling water. Allow it to steep for about 15 minutes.

Bee Balm Salve: Mix 1 tablespoon of bee balm flowers with 8 oz of beeswax. Melt and combine until smooth.

Dosage: Opt for 3-5 cups of bee balm tea daily. The salve can be applied externally as required.

WARNINGS: As with all herbs, excessive consumption can lead to adverse effects. Always stick to recommended dosages and consult a healthcare expert before integrating new herbs into your routine.

Proper identification is crucial. While bee balm has a distinct appearance, there are other plants that might superficially resemble it. Ensure you're harvesting the correct plant to avoid potential health risks.

Birch Tree (Betula sp.)

Plant Name: Birch Tree

Plant Type: Deciduous Tree

Lore: Historically revered for its resilient properties, the birch tree is believed to be one of the first trees to reclaim land after the last ice age. Consequently, it has been endearingly named the 'Pioneer Tree.'

What Does it Treat: Birch bark and twigs are naturally rich in salicylic acid, the same compound found in willow bark and the primary component of aspirin, making it effective in alleviating pain and fever. Furthermore, the leaves and buds of the tree display remarkable antibacterial traits.

Habitat & Region: These trees predominantly flourish in wetlands and in deciduous forests neighboring wetland areas.

Identification:

- **Flowers:** The birch manifests cone-like catkins which transition into samara fruit characterized by their papery wings.
- **Leaves:** Birch leaves are oval in shape and simple, accompanied by toothed or serrated edges.
- **Bark:** A hallmark of the birch is its distinctive, papery, and segmented bark.

Medicinal Parts: While the bark and twigs offer valuable medicinal qualities, the leaves are equally potent, especially as poultices due to their antibacterial attributes.

How to Harvest: A pair of pruners can be efficiently used to sever branches, facilitating the extraction of bark. In the absence of pruners, a fixed-blade knife can accomplish the same. When it comes to collecting leaves, either snip them off with shears or simply detach them using your hands.

Making Medicine:

- Birch Leaf Poultice: Grind birch leaves using a mortar and pestle until they achieve a paste-like consistency. Directly apply this to the wound and secure it with a bandage.

- Birch Bark Hot Infusion: Incorporate 2 oz of birch bark into 1 cup of boiling water. Let it steep for roughly 10 minutes.

Dosage: It's advisable to consume between 2-3 cups of the birch tea or hot infusion daily.

WARNINGS: Identifying trees accurately is paramount. Birch trees share similarities with the beech and alder trees, so it's essential to differentiate between them.

As with any herbal remedy, it's crucial to stick to recommended dosages. Overconsumption can lead to unwanted side effects. Always consult a healthcare professional when integrating new herbal treatments into your routine.

Black Walnut (Juglans nigra)

Plant Name: Black Walnut (Juglans Nigra)

Plant Type: Deciduous Tree

What Does it Treat: Black walnut boasts a range of therapeutic attributes. Notably, the elevated tannin content in the walnut hulls renders it effective for addressing constipation, sore throats, excessive mucus, and even to curtail bleeding.

Habitat & Region: Indigenous to the eastern territories of the United States, black walnut predominantly thrives in wetland ecosystems, particularly in the southeastern regions. Proximity to water sources further enhances its proliferation.

Identification: Mature black walnut trees can attain significant stature. An unmistakable hallmark is the scattering of decaying husks and fragmented walnuts that carpet the ground in its vicinity – a perennial occurrence that even extends to the winter months.

- **Flowers:** Greenish, inconspicuous catkins that dangle, bearing resemblance to grape clusters. They come early but can be hard to see from a distance.
- **Leaves:** Oppositely arranged, the leaves exhibit a blade or dagger-like contour.
- **Nuts:** Despite the mature walnut bearing a characteristic black hue post detachment, it adorns a vivid green shade during its growth phase. This husk, which envelopes the actual nut, is reminiscent of limes or tennis balls when observed on the tree.

Medicinal Parts: The tree bark is the principal source of medicinal potency.

How to Harvest: Gathering walnuts is a relatively straightforward process. To extract the bark, employ a sharp, fixed blade knife.

Making Medicine:

After sun-drying or oven-drying, the hulls can be pulverized into a powder, which when applied to hemorrhaging wounds, capitalizes on the tannins to constrict blood flow, subsequently halting bleeding.

Dosage: For internal maladies such as sore throats and constipation, consuming a cup every couple of hours is advised. Discontinue once relief is achieved. When applied as a fomentation externally, reapply every hour, ceasing once symptoms abate.

WARNINGS:

Black walnut's hulls, foliage, and roots are naturally rich in a compound termed juglone. Elevated concentrations of juglone can prove detrimental. Given its insolubility in water, it permeates the soil in the vicinity of the tree.

Prolonged internal consumption of black walnut preparations is inadvisable. Always seek professional advice before integrating new herbal remedies.

Borage (Borago officinalis)

Plant Name: Borage

Plant Type: Hardy Annual Herbaceous Plant

Lore: With roots in ancient herbology, borage serves multiple purposes in a garden ecosystem. Aside from its ability to thwart hornworms and Japanese beetles, it even enhances strawberry growth.

What Does it Treat: Borage's therapeutic attributes extend to the digestive realm, offering relief for conditions like gastritis, irritable bowel syndrome (IBS), and other similar gastrointestinal disturbances. Borage tea is also traditionally used as a remedy for pneumonia.

Habitat & Region: Borage naturally flourishes in woodlands and pastures. It's a versatile plant, amenable to both wild habitats and cultivated gardens.

Identification: Exhibiting a slightly drooping demeanor, borage is easily distinguishable by its striking blue flowers and fine hair-covered leaves, bestowing it with a soft and fuzzy appearance. The plant usually reaches a height of around 3 feet when fully matured.

- **Flowers:** The flower is particularly eye-catching with its quintet of blue petals arranged in a star pattern.
- **Leaves:** Bearing a semblance to sage, the leaves are large, soft, and distinctly veined.

Medicinal Parts: Borage's medicinal virtues pervade the entirety of the plant.

How to Harvest: Employing a small shovel allows for the whole plant to be harvested. Additionally, shears can be utilized to trim borage as required.

Making Medicine:

- **Borage Tea:** Combine 2oz of borage with 1 cup of boiling water. Allow it to steep for approximately 10 minutes before straining.
- **Borage** Tincture: To create a potent borage tincture, fill a mason jar with fresh borage flowers. Submerge them in vodka, ensuring they are fully covered. Seal the jar and allow it to infuse for 2 to 6 weeks, occasionally shaking.

Dosage: For therapeutic purposes, borage tea can be consumed 2-3 times daily. If using the tincture, 10-15 drops 2-3 times a day is recommended.

WARNINGS: Borage contains small amounts of pyrrolizidine alkaloids which, if consumed in large quantities or over extended periods, might be harmful to the liver. Pregnant and nursing mothers should avoid it. Always consult with a healthcare professional before adding new herbal remedies to your regimen. Additionally, some individuals might be allergic to components of borage, so it's always prudent to initiate any new remedy in small doses to observe any adverse reactions.

Burdock (Arctium lappa)

Plant Name: Burdock

Plant Type: Biennial herbaceous plant commonly considered a "weed"

Lore: Historically cherished by 12th-century herbalists, the burdock plant was venerated for its myriad medicinal properties.

What Does it Treat: A detoxifying agent par excellence, burdock is hailed for its capability to purify the body system – be it the skin, the digestive tract, or even the internal organs.

Habitat & Region: Predominantly seen alongside riverbanks, in disturbed soils, and sun-drenched open fields, burdock has a proclivity for moist environments.

Identification: Burdock is fairly ubiquitous in certain regions. Its distinctive features include expansive frilly leaves and a characteristic purple prickly flower bulb.

- **Flowers:** A distinguishing mark of the burdock plant, the spiky purple flower takes on a vase or gourd shape.
- **Leaves:** Heart-shaped and frilly, these leaves transition from a deep green hue to a pale whitish tone.
- **Roots:** Burdock possesses an elongated taproot that runs deep into the ground.

Medicinal Parts: The taproot is the primary part endowed with medicinal attributes.

How to Harvest: Due to the profound depth of its root, tools like a garden fork or a small shovel would be most effective in uprooting it.

Making Medicine:

- Burdock Root Hot Infusion: Integrate 2oz of sliced burdock root in 1 cup of boiling water. Allow it to steep for approximately 10-15 minutes before filtering.

- Burdock Root Tincture: Slice the burdock root and position them within a mason jar. Fill the jar with 100% alcohol until the root slices are submerged. Seal it tight and store in a cool, dark enclave for 6 weeks.

Dosage: The hot infusion or tea should be consumed 3-5 times per day. The tincture can be administered thrice daily, with each dose being 10ml.

WARNINGS: As with many natural remedies, moderation is key. Pregnant women should refrain from taking large doses of burdock. Additionally, as burdock closely resembles belladonna nightshade – a highly toxic plant – ensure accurate identification prior to harvesting. Always consult with a healthcare professional before incorporating new herbal treatments into your routine.

Calendula (Calendula officinalis)

Plant Name: Calendula

Plant Type: Vibrant and widely cultivated annual flowering plant

Lore: Apart from its therapeutic advantages, calendula also plays a role as a natural dye for fabrics.

What Does it Treat: Recognized for its astringent, antiseptic, and antibiotic attributes, calendula serves as a potent remedy for wound healing. It also proves beneficial for conditions like skin irritations, rashes, and acne. Internally, it can address inflammation and can be used as a mouthwash for oral sores.

Habitat & Region: Indigenous to warmer terrains, calendula thrives in field settings. However, its adaptability makes it an ideal candidate for home gardens, where it is cultivated as a valuable medicinal plant.

Identification: Referred to as pot marigold, this plant is characterized by its radiant golden blossoms.

- **Flowers:** Perched on robust stems, its sizable flowers consist of numerous petals surrounding a yellow core.
- **Leaves:** Resembling the dandelion leaves but without the serrated edges, the basal leaves of calendula are rounder and broaden towards the tip.

Medicinal Parts: The petals of the calendula bloom are highly esteemed for their therapeutic properties.

How to Harvest: Calendula flowers can be easily severed using shears. They can be air-dried traditionally or used immediately.

Making Medicine:

- Infused Calendula Oil: Loosely pack a mason jar with calendula petals. Drench them in a carrier oil such as avocado or almond oil. Expose the jar to direct sunlight for a week. Subsequently, strain the contents. The resultant oil can be applied topically.

- Calendula Hot Infusion and Tea: Immerse the petals from half a calendula flower in 1 cup of boiling water. Let it steep for approximately 10 minutes.

Dosage: Calendula's bitter taste often limits its dosage. Nonetheless, it remains a potent remedy. Apply the infused oil sparingly on the affected areas.

Consume the tea in moderation, restricting to a maximum of two doses daily.

WARNINGS: Calendula belongs to the Asteraceae family, analogous to daisies. Consequently, it can trigger allergic reactions in susceptible individuals. Hence, it's prudent to commence with small amounts to assess tolerance and gradually increase the dosage if no allergic reactions are observed. Always consult with a healthcare professional when introducing new medicinal plants into your regimen.

Cayenne (Capsicum annuum)

Plant Name: Cayenne Pepper

Plant Type: Annual Pepper Plant

Habitat & Region: Cayenne peppers flourish in garden environments, especially under bounteous sunlight. They are native to tropical areas but are cultivated worldwide.

Identification: Cayenne pepper plants bear a resemblance to other pepper cultivars but produce distinct, elongated, crinkled red peppers known for their spiciness.

- **Flowers:** Before transitioning into the pepper fruit, the plant produces a white bloom with sharp-edged petals.
- **Leaves:** Akin to other pepper species, Cayenne's leaves are elliptical and taper to a pointed tip.
- **Fruits:** Initially green, the Cayenne pepper undergoes a color transformation, ripening into a vibrant red hue. It is characterized by its slender, elongated shape.

Medicinal Parts: The primary therapeutic component of the plant is the pepper fruit itself.

How to Harvest: Upon ripening, peppers can be gently plucked or sheared from the stem.

What Does it Treat: Renowned for its therapeutic properties, Cayenne pepper aids in the digestive process, clears congested sinuses, and showcases antiviral and antibacterial characteristics. Additionally, it acts as an energy booster. An interesting application of powdered cayenne is its ability to arrest bleeding when applied directly to wounds.

Making Medicine: The most prevalent form of medicinal cayenne is its powdered version.

Dosage: For internal use, mix 1 tsp of cayenne powder into a glass of water.

WARNINGS: Cayenne is typically safe for most individuals. However, excessive consumption can lead to stomach discomfort and a burning sensation. Topical application may cause irritation for some; it's recommended to conduct a patch test beforehand. Always ensure you are cultivating and consuming the intended pepper variety. Some individuals might be sensitive to the spice, so moderation is recommended. Always consult with a healthcare professional before adding new medicinal plants or supplements to your regimen.

Cherry

Plant Name: Cherry

Plant Type: Tree

Habitat & Region: Wild cherry predominantly occupies the eastern half of the United States, boasting a vast habitat.

Identification: Wild cherry trees offer two distinct identification markers:

- **Fruits:** They bear clusters of cherries annually, with each cherry resembling the size of a small blueberry. These cherries can vary in color from black to red and dangle from elongated stems.
- **Bark:** When a segment of the bark is detached, it exudes a pronounced cherry aroma, unmistakably indicative of the tree's identity.
- **Flowers:** Wild cherry blossoms are either white or pink in hue, presenting themselves as petite, delicate blooms adorned with extended stamens.
- **Leaves:** The tree's foliage is reminiscent of birch leaves - a clover shape that tapers into a point at the ends.

Medicinal Parts: Both the outer bark and the fruits of the tree are harvested for medicinal purposes.

How to Harvest: It's crucial to avoid the tree's leaves and stems, as they contain toxic compounds. Ensure only the bark and cherries are harvested, ensuring that the cherries are devoid of stems.

What Does it Treat: Wild cherry serves as a potent expectorant and proves to be effective against symptoms related to colds and coughs.

Making Medicine:

1. **Cherry Juice:**
   - Harvest mature cherries, ensuring they are free from stems.
   - Wash the cherries thoroughly under cool water.
   - Using a juicer or a mortar and pestle, extract the juice from the cherries. If you're using a mortar and pestle, make sure to strain the juice to remove any solid fragments.
   - Store in a cool place. Consume as recommended.

2. **Wild Cherry Bark Infusion:**

- Harvest the outer bark of the cherry tree.

- Thoroughly clean the bark to remove any dirt or contaminants.

- For a single cup of infusion, take about 1-2 teaspoons of chopped or shredded bark.

- Boil water, and pour it over the bark.

- Allow the mixture to steep for about 10 minutes.

- Strain the liquid, removing the bark.

- The infusion can now be consumed. It's best taken warm.

Dosage:

Cherry Juice: Consume as needed, but always in moderation given its tartness and potency.

Wild Cherry Bark Infusion: It's advised not to exceed an intake of 3 cups per day.

WARNINGS: The wild cherry tree has several components that are toxic. Overconsumption or inappropriate usage can lead to adverse effects. It's paramount to exclusively use the bark and the cherry fruits for medicinal purposes. Always consult with a healthcare professional before using any medicinal plants.

Chamomile (Matricaria recutita and Anthemis nobilis)

Plant Name: Chamomile

Plant Type: Flowering Plant

Habitat & Region: Chamomile is adaptable and flourishes in various conditions due to the different habitat preferences of its varieties. German chamomile thrives in poor draining clay soils and can tolerate some shade, making it more versatile. On the other hand, Roman chamomile prefers well-drained soils and requires ample sunlight. Open prairies or meadows are ideal locations to spot these plants.

Identification: Chamomile is distinguished by its daisy-like flowers.

- **Flowers:** These have creamy white petals that surround a prominent, bright yellow, cone-shaped center.
- **Leaves:** Feather-like and delicate, the leaves primarily grow at the base of the plant.

Medicinal Parts: The primary medicinal components of chamomile are its flowers and leaves. Both can be consumed and are often used in herbal remedies.

How to Harvest: Carefully snip the flower heads and leaves using garden shears or scissors, ensuring you don't pull or damage the plant's roots.

What Does it Treat? Chamomile is renowned for its calming properties. It can help alleviate symptoms of anxiety and insomnia. Consuming chamomile tea or a hot infusion before bedtime can promote relaxation and a good night's sleep.

Making Medicine: Chamomile can be utilized in various medicinal preparations, including:

- Hot Infusion/Tea: Use about 1-2 teaspoons of fresh or dried chamomile per cup of boiling water. Allow to steep for about 5-10 minutes.
- Tinctures: A concentrated extract made by soaking the herb in alcohol.
- Baths: Adding chamomile flowers to your bath can provide a soothing experience.

Dosage: Being a mild herb, chamomile can be consumed in regular amounts. However, its sedative properties make it ideal for evening use to aid relaxation and sleep.

WARNINGS (high dose dangerous, dangerous lookalikes): While chamomile is generally safe, it belongs to the Asteraceae family. Individuals allergic to plants in this family, like ragweed, marigolds, or daisies, might react to chamomile. Always conduct an allergy patch test when trying a new herbal remedy. Moreover, while there are no toxic plants that closely resemble chamomile, always ensure correct identification before consumption

Red Clover (Trifolium pratense)

Plant Name: Red Clover

Plant Type: Ground Cover

Habitat & Region: Red clover is adaptable and can be found thriving in various environments including grassy prairies, disturbed grounds, both front and backyards, sunny pathways, and other areas dominated by ground cover plants.

Identification: Red clover is often mistaken for the four-leaf clover, though it typically does not produce the famed four leaves.

- **Flowers:** Its flowers are pinkish to purplish, aggregated into a rounded, slightly bristly flower head.
- **Leaves:** Each trifoliate (three-parted) leaf displays a characteristic white V marking. As the plant matures, the leaves might elongate and take on a more oval shape.

Medicinal Parts: The flower head of the red clover is the primary part used for its medicinal benefits.

How to Harvest: Gently pinch off the flower heads with your fingers. They detach quite easily.

What Does it Treat: Red clover acts as an effective expectorant, beneficial for alleviating allergies and asthma symptoms. Notably, it offers significant benefits to women; it contains compounds that support milk production during breastfeeding and can help mitigate menopausal symptoms.

Making Medicine:

- Hot Infusion/Tea: To prepare a tea using dried red clover flowers, steep 1 teaspoon of the dried flowers in 1 cup of hot water for 10 minutes. Strain and enjoy.

- If using fresh flowers, utilize 1 tablespoon of fresh blossoms in 3 ½ cups of boiling water. Cover and steep for 10 minutes. Strain before drinking.

Dosage: For best results, consume red clover tea 2-3 times daily when experiencing symptoms.

WARNINGS (high dose dangerous, dangerous lookalikes): Women who are pregnant or those on birth control pills should avoid consuming red clover tea due to its potential hormonal effects. Always ensure you're correctly identifying red clover and not confusing it with other similar-looking plants.

Comfrey (Symphytum officinale)

Plant Name: Comfrey

Plant Type: This is a rough-leaved, tall perennial.

Lore: Historically, soldiers in the 1950s would sometimes arrive at the Royal Hospital of Sheffield in England with broken limbs wrapped in comfrey leaves, attesting to the plant's traditional medicinal uses.

What Does it Treat: Comfrey is primarily used topically for skin issues such as scratches, burns, sunburns, and minor wounds. Its mucilaginous leaves and roots can also be consumed as they're believed to help with coughs and respiratory problems.

Habitat & Region: Comfrey prefers old fields and areas that are uncultivated or waste areas.

Identification: This flowering perennial stands tall and is easily recognizable by its purple flowers and distinctive bristly leaves.

- **Flowers:** These bell-shaped, purple flowers are quite distinctive.
- **Leaves:** The bristly green leaves are larger at the plant's base. These leaves are also prominently veined.
- **Roots:** Comfrey's root runs deep, and even a small fragment of it can rejuvenate the entire plant.

Medicinal Parts: Both the leaves and roots of comfrey are used for medicinal purposes.

How to Harvest: Use shears to trim the leaves when they are visible. To harvest the roots, wait until after the last frost or once the plant has died back in the winter. Employ a hori hori or similar tool for digging up the roots. Ensure both leaves and roots are dried before medicinal use.

Making Medicine:

- **Comfrey Hot Infusion/Tea:** Steep 2oz of comfrey in 1 cup of water for about 10 minutes.
- **Comfrey Salve and Oil:** These can be made from the leaves and are perfect for direct skin application.
- **Comfrey Root Decoction:** Use 1 teaspoon of dried root per 1 cup of water. Simmer for about 5-6 minutes and strain before drinking.

Dosage: Comfrey tea can be consumed 3-4 times daily. The decoction made from comfrey root can be had 2-3 times a day.

WARNINGS: While comfrey has traditional medicinal uses, it also contains compounds (pyrrolizidine alkaloids) that can be toxic when consumed in large amounts or over extended periods. It is recommended to seek guidance from a qualified herbalist or medical professional before using comfrey internally. Additionally, it's important not to apply comfrey to deep or puncture wounds.

Cornflower (Centaurea cyanus)

Plant Name: Cornflower

Plant Type: An ornamental Flowering Herb

Lore: Historically, the cornflower was donned by men who were in love. A rapid fading of the flower's color would prompt the man to reconsider the depth of his emotions. Cornflowers were also used as a natural dye.

What Does it Treat: Cornflower is renowned for its anti-inflammatory properties, which can be attributed to a potent compound it contains known as anthocyanin. This compound is a robust anti-inflammatory and antioxidant. Internally, cornflower can help address conditions like stomach ulcers. When applied topically, it is beneficial for rashes and conditions like eczema.

Habitat & Region: Prefers well-drained, nutrition-rich sandy soils.

Identification: A typically multi-stemmed plant, the cornflower stands anywhere between 1 to 3 feet tall, boasting a vivid blue hue.

- **Flowers:** These unique, spiky blue flowers bloom from June through August and form a circle of florets.
- **Leaves:** While the stems adopt a grey-green color, the leaves are initially long, becoming more grass-like as the plant ages.

Medicinal Parts: The flower petals of the cornflower are primarily used for medicinal purposes.

How to Harvest: To dry the cornflowers, trim the stems and suspend the flowers upside-down in a well-ventilated area.

Making Medicine:

- **Cornflower Hot Infusion/Tea:** Use 2oz of cornflower petals for every cup of water, steeping the blend for 10 minutes.

- **Cornflower Salve:** Melt 8oz of beeswax and stir in 1 tablespoon of cornflower petals.

Dosage: Cornflower tea can be consumed 3-5 times daily. The cornflower salve can be applied topically as needed.WARNINGS (high dose dangerous, dangerous lookalikes)

WARNINGS: Cornflowers, while safe for most, can cause allergic reactions in some individuals, especially when applied to the skin. Always do a patch test before extensive topical application. Always ensure correct identification of plants before consumption or use, as there are other blue flowering plants that may look similar but are not safe for ingestion or application.

Daisy (Bellis perennis)

Plant Name: Daisy

Plant Type: "Tender Perennial" Flower

Lore: Across cultures, the daisy symbolizes various significant themes. In Christianity, it embodies the innocence of both Christ as a child and the Virgin Mary. Native American traditions see it as a representation of the sun. Meanwhile, in Norse mythology, the daisy stands for fertility.

What Does it Treat: The daisy is versatile in its medicinal properties. It can act as a coagulant to stem bleeding, aid in digestion, alleviate coughs, and even help relieve back pain.

Habitat & Region: Daisies thrive in meadows and grassland environments.

Identification: A daisy is easy to spot, with a single flower atop each dark green stalk. The leaves are blunt and oblong, making this common flower recognizable to many.

- **Flowers:** The outer florets can be either white or yellow, while the inner florets can vary between white and yellow.
- **Leaves:** These are dark green, blunt, and oblong.
- **Roots:** The daisy has a creeping root system.

Medicinal Parts: The whole part of the plant that is above the ground, including flowers and leaves, can be utilized for its medicinal benefits.

How to Harvest: For the best yield, trim the stalks of the daisy.

Making Medicine: Daisy Hot Infusion: Combine 1 tablespoon of daisy flowers and leaves with 1 cup of water. Allow this to steep for around 10 minutes.

Dosage: Drink 2-3 cups of the daisy hot infusion daily.

WARNINGS: Some individuals may be allergic to daisies. Always conduct a patch test or consume a small amount first to ensure you don't have an allergic reaction. While daisies are generally safe for most people, consuming in excessive amounts may cause side effects. Always adhere to the recommended dosage. The common daisy is distinct, but ensure that you are identifying it correctly. There are many similar-looking plants, and some of them might not be safe for consumption or application.

Dandelion (Taraxacum officinale)

Plant Name: Dandelion

Plant Type: Herbaceous Perennial Flowering "Weed"

Habitat & Region: Dandelions are versatile and can be found in meadows, pastures, and even residential lawns.

Identification: The dandelion is commonly dismissed as a mere weed. However, its edible leaves and iconic bright yellow flowers were traditionally treasured for their medicinal and culinary properties.

- **Flowers:** Vibrant yellow and multi-petaled, these flowers are a hallmark of the dandelion.
- **Leaves:** Young leaves are tender with a distinct serrated edge and lie flat on the ground. They become spiny with maturity.

Medicinal Parts: The dandelion's leaves, flowers, and roots all have medicinal attributes.

How to Harvest: Dandelions can be plucked by hand, but for a more efficient collection, use kitchen shears.

Therapeutic Uses: Dandelions have been traditionally used as diuretics, aids in digestion, and treatments for minor skin ailments like acne and eczema.

Making Medicine:

- **Dandelion Tea:** For a simple tea, steep 1-2 teaspoons of dried dandelion leaves, flowers, or roots in a cup of boiling water for 10 minutes. Strain and drink.

- **Dandelion Tincture:** Fill a jar with fresh dandelion flowers, leaves, and roots. Cover completely with a high-proof alcohol like vodka. Seal and store in a cool, dark place for 4-6 weeks, shaking daily. Strain the herbs out, and store the tincture in a dark glass bottle. Take a few drops to a teaspoon as needed, either directly or diluted in water.

- **Dandelion Salve (for skin):** Infuse dried dandelion flowers in a carrier oil (like olive or coconut oil) in a jar for 2-3 weeks, shaking daily. Strain out the flowers, then gently heat the oil and mix with melted beeswax at a ratio of 4 parts oil to 1 part beeswax. Pour into tins or jars and allow to cool. Apply to affected areas of the skin as needed.

Dosage: Drink 1 cup of dandelion tea up to three times daily. Use the dandelion salve on affected areas as necessary.

WARNINGS: Overconsumption of dandelion can lead to stomach discomfort. Confirm you are correctly identifying dandelions, as there are plants with a similar appearance. Always harvest with certainty. Pregnant or breastfeeding women should consult a healthcare professional before using dandelion or any other medicinal herbs.

Echinacea (Echinacea purpurea)

Plant Name: Echinacea

Plant Type: Herbaceous Perennial Plant

Habitat & Region: Echinacea thrives in dry open woods, prairies that support wildflowers, and disturbed grounds. It is native to North America.

Identification: Echinacea, also known as the purple coneflower, stands out with its striking purple-pink petals and dark orange center. Plants can grow up to 3 feet in height.

- **Flowers:** Typically purple or pink with a pronounced dark orange center resembling a cone.
- **Leaves:** These are textured, and have a lanceolate or spear-pointed shape. Prior to flowering, the plant can be identified by stalks with these leaves.

Medicinal Parts: The leaves, flowers, roots, and stems are all sought after for their medicinal attributes.

How to Harvest: Use shears or small pruners to clip the flowers or leaves. If not being used immediately, hang them upside down in a dry, well-ventilated area to dry.

Making Medicine:
- Echinacea Tea (Infusion): Steep 1-2 teaspoons of dried echinacea parts (leaves, flowers, or roots) in boiling water for 15 minutes. Strain and drink.

- Cold Infusion: Soak the echinacea parts in cold water for several hours, then strain and drink.

- Echinacea Tincture: Fill a jar with echinacea parts and cover them with high-proof alcohol (like vodka). Seal the jar, and let it sit in a cool, dark place for 4-6 weeks, shaking occasionally. Strain out the plant material, and store the tincture in a dark glass bottle. This concentrated form is taken in drop dosages.

Dosage: For boosting immunity or fighting cold symptoms, drink echinacea tea or take the tincture 2-3 times daily.

WARNINGS: Overuse or prolonged use of echinacea might lead to side effects like stomach upset or rashes. Individuals allergic to plants in the Asteraceae family should avoid echinacea. Always ensure correct identification of echinacea, as there are other plants with similar-looking flowers. It's important for

pregnant or breastfeeding women, or individuals with autoimmune disorders, to consult a healthcare professional before using echinacea or any medicinal herb.

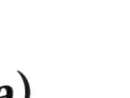

Elderberry (Sambucus nigra)

Plant Name: Elderberry

Plant Type: Large Deciduous Shrub

Lore: Remnants of elderberry seeds from the Neolithic period were discovered in Swiss dwellings, attesting to its longstanding relationship with humans.

What Does it Treat: Elderberry's potent antiviral properties make it a popular remedy for the flu. Its high Vitamin C content boosts immunity. Additionally, elderberry can alleviate constipation, sinus infections, headaches, and more.

Habitat & Region: Elderberry thrives in humid wetlands and at forest edges.

Identification: The elderberry plant showcases a distinct transition from young green shoots to older, woody stems, which can reach up to 7 feet in height. These stems sprout clusters of white flowers that yield dark purple berries.

- **Flowers:** White, fragrant, and clustered in umbrella-shaped formations.
- **Leaves:** Lanceolate or spear-shaped with pronounced veins and serrated edges.
- **Berries:** Start as green but mature into a dark purple.

Medicinal Parts: Both the berries and flowers possess medicinal properties.

How to Harvest: Using shears, snip off the clusters of ripe elderberries. If harvesting flowers, do so before the berries form.

Making Medicine: Elderberry Syrup:

1. **Ingredients:**

- 6 Cups Elderberries
- 1/3 Cup Honey
- 1 Inch Cinnamon Stick
- 1 Whole Clove
- 3 slices of Lemon

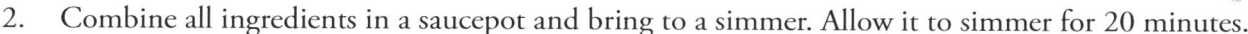

2. Combine all ingredients in a saucepot and bring to a simmer. Allow it to simmer for 20 minutes.

3. Strain the mixture, pressing the berries to extract as much juice as possible.

4. Transfer the syrup to glass bottles and store in the refrigerator or can in a hot water canner for longer storage.

Dosage: Consume 1 tablespoon of elderberry syrup three times daily.

WARNINGS: Only the flowers and berries of the elderberry plant are safe for consumption. All other parts, including stems and leaves, are toxic and can lead to nausea, vomiting, and more severe symptoms when ingested. Ensure you are picking true elderberry, as there are other berry-producing plants that can be toxic.

Evening Primrose (Oenothera biennis)

Plant Name: Evening Primrose

Plant Type: Biennial Wildflower

Lore: Historically, Druids held primrose in their possession to protect against malevolent forces.

What Does it Treat: Evening Primrose is utilized for addressing skin inflammation and arthritis.

Habitat & Region: The plant thrives in prairies, alongside field edges, and in areas that exhibit disturbed soil.

Identification: Evening Primrose is recognized by its clustered yellow blooms on green stems, anchored by lanceolate leaves.

- **Flowers:** Bearing a resemblance to clover, its yellow blooms consist of 4 heart-shaped petals.
- **Leaves:** The plant showcases dark green leaves, sometimes toothed, that form primarily at its base.

Medicinal Parts: Every component of the Evening Primrose possesses medicinal properties.

How to Harvest: Harvest the seeds, flower buds, and leaves throughout the year. If targeting the roots, harvest prior to the plant flowering.

Making Medicine: Primrose Flower Oil:

1. Take a mason jar and layer it with unblemished evening primrose flower petals.

2. Submerge the petals in a carrier oil such as olive or grapeseed oil, ensuring no air remains.

3. Secure with a sterilized lid and let it rest for approximately two weeks. Daily gentle shaking is beneficial.

4. Following the two weeks, your oil is primed for usage.

Dosage: The oil is suitable for internal consumption once a day. A maximum of two teaspoons is advisable. Its nutty, pleasant taste complements salads when used as a dressing.

WARNINGS:

- Excessive dosing can lead to Primrose poisoning.

- It's paramount for individuals with epilepsy to approach Evening Primrose with caution due to potential adverse reactions.

Feverfew (Tanacetum parthenium)

Plant Name: Feverfew

Plant Type: Perennial Shrub

Lore: Historically, Feverfew was regarded as a symbol of good fortune. Travelers often carried it with them, believing it would bring them luck on their journeys.

What Does it Treat: Feverfew possesses anti-inflammatory properties. It's commonly utilized for ailments such as migraines, arthritis, fevers, and the common cold.

Habitat & Region: This plant has a preference for mountainous scrublands, old fields, and waste areas.

Identification: Feverfew grows in clumps, creating mounded structures. The shrub blooms with several daisy-like florets with white petals, which are accompanied by feathery, fern-like leaves.

- **Flowers:** From June to September, the plant sports daisy-like white flowers.
- **Leaves:** These leaves, similar in appearance to parsley, are feathery with a light fuzz.

Medicinal Parts: While the leaves can be chewed, one should exercise caution due to the potential for skin irritation.

How to Harvest: Both leaves and flowers of the feverfew plant can be harvested. While the leaves can be taken at any time, the flowers should be plucked at their peak bloom.

Making Medicine: Feverfew Hot Infusion and Tea:

1. Add 1 teaspoon of feverfew leaves and flowers to a cup.
2. Pour in boiling water.
3. Allow the mixture to steep for about 10 minutes.
4. Strain and serve.

Dosage: It's recommended to consume no more than 3 cups of this infusion per day.

WARNINGS (high dose dangerous, dangerous lookalikes)

- Direct contact with the leaves may lead to skin irritation in sensitive individuals.

- Pregnant individuals should refrain from consuming feverfew tea.

- Those allergic to ragweed or similar plants should exercise caution when considering feverfew due to potential allergic reactions.

Garlic (Allium sativum)

Plant Name: Garlic

Plant Type: Perennial Herb

Lore: According to old gardener folklore, rabbits were believed to avoid crossing boundaries lined with garlic.

What Does it Treat: Garlic is often seen as a versatile remedy. It's known for reducing cholesterol and high blood pressure, and also boasts antibiotic, antiseptic, antifungal, and antiviral properties.

Habitat & Region: Ideally grows in deciduous fields and woodlands, especially in the proximity of moist areas like creeks or swamps.

Identification: Wild garlic sprouts in clusters with lengthy, lanceolate leaves. The distinct garlic odor from its root and its small white flowers are its identifying features.

- **Flowers:** Bearing a globe shape, these white flowers, with 5 to 6 petals, are enveloped in pale green stems prior to blossoming.
- **Leaves:** These broad, lanceolate leaves, lying closer to the ground, arch back to the earth.

Medicinal Parts: The entirety of the plant is both edible and medicinal. However, the root stands out due to its potency and widespread use.

How to Harvest: The prime time to harvest wild garlic is in spring. By midsummer, its leaves enter dormancy, rendering the plant more elusive. When foraging, utilize tools like a small shovel or hori hori knife, and ensure you practice sustainable harvesting.

Making Medicine: Wild Garlic Salve: This easy-to-make salve involves blending the ingredients and then straining the mixture. Ingredients:

- 1/2 cup coconut oil
- 2 tablespoons olive oil
- 8 cloves peeled, raw wild garlic
- 5 drops of Oregano Oil

Dosage: To reap its benefits, rub the salve onto the chest for alleviating coughs, apply to the soles for bloodstream absorption, or put on wounds for sanitization and quicker healing.

WARNINGS: Beware of look-alikes! The Lily of the Valley bears a striking resemblance to wild garlic but is toxic. However, unlike garlic, it doesn't emit a strong garlic aroma, which is a distinguishing factor. Always ensure you're harvesting the right plant, and when in doubt, consult an expert or refrain from consumption.

Ginger (Zingiber officinale)

Plant Name: Ginger

Plant Type: Rhizomatous Herb

Lore: A bath infused with ginger slices is believed to amplify the Divine Masculine Energy, promoting assertiveness and concentration.

What Does it Treat: Boasting an array of healing properties, ginger aids in boosting blood circulation and reducing inflammation. This can alleviate sore muscles, internal and external swelling, cough suppression, cold symptoms, and even motion sickness. Truly, ginger is a versatile remedy!

Habitat & Region: Ginger thrives in environments offering partial to full shade, often alongside deciduous trees and in acidic soils. It's commonly found in the Eastern United States.

Identification: Wild ginger typically grows in clusters, with a height no greater than 6 inches. It showcases heart-shaped, dark green leaves and a unique flower, brown to purple in color, comprising of three sepals and devoid of petals.

- **Flowers:** Brown or purplish, these flowers are characterized by three thick, yet dry sepals.
- **Leaves:** These heart or kidney-shaped leaves are veined and possess a dark green hue. They are never triangular.
- **Roots:** Smaller compared to cultivated ginger. However, when scratched, they emit the characteristic ginger aroma.

Medicinal Parts: The root is the primary medicinal part.

How to Harvest: Wild ginger roots can be harvested throughout the year. Using a hori hori knife or a small shovel, one can easily extract the roots.

Making Medicine: Fresh Ginger Tea: A popular remedy, ginger tea offers many benefits. To prepare, steep a finger-length ginger root in 2 cups of boiling water for 8-10 minutes. Enhance the flavor by adding honey and lemon to taste.

Dosage: You can indulge in this tea as often as you desire!

WARNINGS: Be cautious of lookalikes! Hexastylis arifolia resembles wild ginger, especially with its triangular leaves and purplish flowers. Always ensure correct identification before consumption and consult an expert if uncertain.

Ginseng (Panax sp.)

Plant Name: Ginseng (Note: Ginseng is threatened or endangered in many states)

Plant Type: Perennial Herb

Lore: Ginseng's reputation as a potent herb dates back to the Han Dynasty (206 BC-220 AD), during which only royalty could consume it. This was due to its legendary effects on longevity, health, and virility.

What Does it Treat: A long-cherished remedy, ginseng is celebrated for its ability to energize the body, heighten focus, and mitigate the impacts of stress.

Habitat & Region: Prefers north-facing slopes in deciduous forests, predominantly found in the Appalachia and Ozarks.

Identification: The distinct American ginseng features a primary stem that births 4-5 branch stems. These stems are adorned with five, 3-pronged, leaflets.

- **Roots:** Ginseng roots often mimic a humanoid form, earning it the nickname 'Man Root'.
- **Leaves:** Bright and prominent, the five leaves of ginseng consist of three larger ones and two smaller ones, distinguishing them from other forest plants.
- **Berries:** Centered on the primary stalk is a single cluster of red berries.

Medicinal Parts: The roots are the primary medicinal parts.

How to Harvest: Using tools like a hori hori knife or a small shovel, carefully dig around the ginseng root, ensuring minimal disturbance and then extract it.

Making Medicine: Ginseng Tea: To harness the power of ginseng, steep ½ teaspoon of dried root in 8 oz of hot water for 3-5 minutes. Sweeten with honey if desired.

Dosage: To reap its benefits, drink ginseng tea 2-3 times daily, preferably between meals.

WARNINGS: The importance of sustainable harvesting cannot be overstated, especially for a plant as precious as wild ginseng. Ensure you're using eco-friendly methods when foraging to protect the longevity of this remarkable medicinal herb. Always be certain of the plant's identity, and consult with experts to prevent over-harvesting or confusion with lookalikes.

Goldenseal (Hydrastis canadensis)

Plant Name: Goldenseal

Plant Type: Perennial Herb

Lore: With its multifaceted uses, Goldenseal has garnered a plethora of names reflecting its rich history, including Indian dye, yellow root, ground raspberry, yellow puccoon, wild curcuma, eye root, eye-balm, yellow paint, wild turmeric, and yelloweye.

What Does it Treat: Goldenseal has traditionally been employed to manage colds, upper respiratory tract ailments, various skin concerns, ulcers, and even vaginitis.

Habitat & Region: It thrives predominantly in the shaded forests of the southern regions.

Identification: Goldenseal stands at a height of about 10-20 inches and possesses a singular, hairy stem crowned with two palmate leaves.

- **Flowers:** Unlike many other plants, Goldenseal's flowers lack petals. Each plant yields a singular flower characterized by three light green sepals.
- **Leaves:** Bearing a resemblance to maple, the palmate leaves showcase 5-9 points and have jagged edges.

Medicinal Parts: The medicinal qualities reside predominantly in the above-ground parts of the plant.

How to Harvest: Utilize shears to carefully cut and collect Goldenseal without damaging the plant.

Making Medicine: Goldenseal Tincture:

- Ratio: 1:2 (1 cup of herbs to 2 cups of 40% alcohol).
- Once the herbs are soaked in alcohol for several weeks, strain out the plant material. Store in a cool, dark place.

Dosage: Ingest 1 teaspoon per day. Given its intense bitterness, dilution with water or a beverage is recommended.

WARNINGS: Goldenseal can be potent. Overconsumption may lead to digestive upset, nervous system issues, or other side effects. It's also not recommended for pregnant or breastfeeding women.

Hawthorn (Crataegus sp.)

Plant Name: Hawthorn

Plant Type: Flowering Shrub

Lore: Hawthorn's rich history dates back to an astonishing 15 million years, with fossilized evidence indicating its existence during the Miocene period.

What Does it Treat: Primarily renowned for its cardiovascular benefits, Hawthorn plays a pivotal role in treating high blood pressure and other heart-related conditions.

Habitat & Region: It flourishes in deciduous woodlands.

Identification: Although a slow grower, with patience, the Hawthorn tree can stretch up to 13 feet, though reaching this height could span anywhere between 25-50 years. Its bark stands out with its deep fissures and unique grey-green hue.

- **Flowers:** Hawthorn showcases elegant white flowers with five petals that sprout from a distinct pinkish stem.
- **Leaves:** With a trio of lobes, Hawthorn leaves are elongated and sport a tough texture.
- **Fruit:** As autumn graces the landscape, Hawthorn trees become adorned with dark red, round berries.

Medicinal Parts: The berries are the star when it comes to Hawthorn's therapeutic properties.

How to Harvest: Berries can either be plucked individually by hand or, for a more efficient approach, entire clusters can be pruned from the tree.

Making Medicine: Hawthorn Tincture:

- Ratio: 1:2 (1 cup of fresh Hawthorn berries to 2 cups of 60% alcohol).

- Once infused for several weeks, strain out the berries and store the liquid in a cool, dark place.

Dosage: Administer half a teaspoon or approximately half an ounce daily for optimal results.

WARNINGS: Consuming Hawthorn in excessive amounts may lead to low blood pressure and dizziness. It is essential to consult with a healthcare professional before incorporating Hawthorn into your regimen, especially if you are on medications or have heart-related conditions.

Hazelnut Tree (Corylus sp.)

Plant Name: Hazelnut Tree

Plant Type: Deciduous Nut Producing Tree

Lore: For centuries, the hazelnut and its tree have been emblematic symbols of wisdom across various mythologies and cultures, its presence often signaling profound insight and knowledge.

What Does it Treat: The oil derived from hazelnuts offers an array of dermatological benefits. It serves as a protective barrier against sun damage, boasts anti-aging properties, helps combat acne, and even facilitates wound healing.

Habitat & Region: Flourishing in both deciduous and mixed forests, hazelnuts particularly favor proximity to water bodies.

Identification: The hazelnut tree's appearance can be somewhat eclectic, with some manifesting in the traditional tree form while others possess multiple slender, cane-like trunks. Regardless of its form, the tree never ceases to produce its coveted nuts.

- **Flowers:** Distinctive catkins form on the tree. Initially, they are short and green, elongating as they mature.
- **Leaves:** Their leaves are primarily oval with a rounded point, resembling a tail at the end.
- **Nuts:** Nestled in green, semi-translucent husks that transition to a brown brittle texture as they age, hazelnuts not only provide therapeutic benefits but are also a nutritious culinary staple, celebrated for their protein content.

Medicinal Parts: The tree's nuts.

How to Harvest: When the calendar ushers in the early days of fall, hazelnuts signal their readiness for harvest.

Making Medicine: Hazelnut Oil:

- Grind ¼ cup of hazelnuts.

- Combine with 2 cups of either coconut or olive oil.

- Using a double boiler, gently heat the mixture until the temperature reaches about 110 degrees Fahrenheit.

- Allow the concoction to cool entirely before straining it to obtain the pure oil.

Dosage: Gently massage the oil onto the affected skin area.

WARNINGS: Hazelnuts, being tree nuts, may trigger allergic reactions in susceptible individuals. It's imperative to conduct a patch test by applying a minimal amount of hazelnut oil to a small skin area and observing for any adverse reactions. Always consult a healthcare professional before using any new remedy.

Horse Chestnut (Aesculus hippocastanum)

Plant Name: Horse Chestnut

Plant Type: Deciduous Tree

Lore: Dubbed "conkers" in certain parts of the world, horse chestnuts have a peculiar tradition of being kept in corners of rooms, with some believing they deter spiders from taking up residence.

What Does it Treat: A renowned remedy for skin complaints, the horse chestnut is particularly effective in treating varicose veins.

Habitat & Region: These trees make their home in deciduous forests across North America.

Identification: Distinguished by its unique features, the horse chestnut tree boasts spiny chestnuts, arresting clusters of flowers, and its distinctive paw print-like leaves.

- **Flowers:** : Spring sees the horse chestnut bursting into bloom, with cone-shaped clusters of white and pink flowers gracing its branches.
- **Leaves:** The palmate leaves of the horse chestnut, arranged in groups of seven, are characterized by serrated edges. The most prominent leaf, sitting furthest from the stem, is rounded at the apex.
- **Bark:** With age, these trees develop a fluted trunk. The bark is gray-green and prominently fissured.

Medicinal Parts: The medicinal properties of the tree reside in its chestnuts.

How to Harvest: Come autumn, the ground beneath the tree becomes littered with ripened chestnuts. These can be gathered from the ground or plucked directly from the tree.

Making Medicine: Horse Chestnut Oil:

- Grind ¼ cup of horse chestnuts.
- Merge the ground chestnuts with 2 cups of coconut or olive oil.
- Employing a double boiler, heat the blend till the oil reaches approximately 110 degrees Fahrenheit.
- Post heating, let the oil cool to room temperature. Once cooled, strain to separate the liquid from the solids.

Dosage: For external use only, apply the oil to affected areas such as varicose veins, inflamed or itchy skin patches, or muscles prone to cramping.

WARNINGS: It's crucial to note that raw horse chestnuts are highly toxic and can be lethal when consumed. Always exercise caution, ensuring they're kept out of the reach of children and pets, and are not mistaken for edible chestnuts. Before using any new remedy, it's wise to seek advice from a healthcare professional.

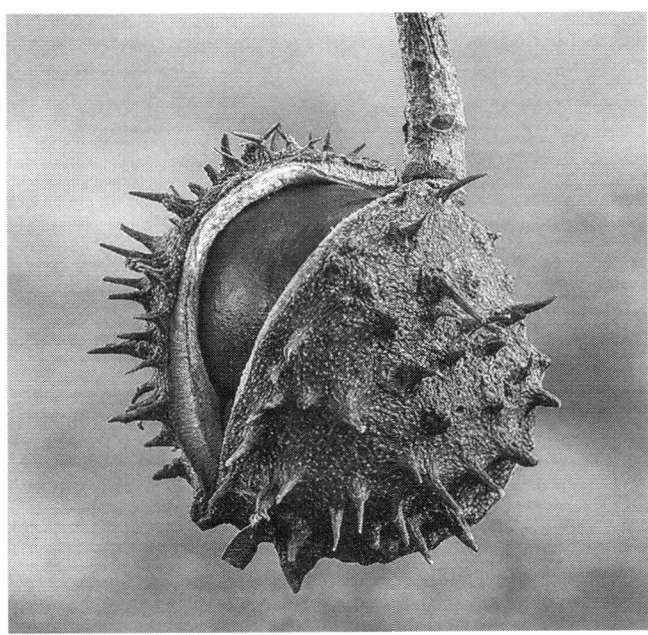

Horsetail (Equisetum arvense)

Plant Name: Horsetail

Plant Type: Perennial Grasslike Plant

Lore: The ancient Romans found utility in horsetail's rough, rigid exterior, employing mature horsetail as a pot scrubber.

What Does it Treat: Renowned for its high silica content, horsetail is a go-to for wound healing. Beyond that, it offers relief to those grappling with arthritis and serves as an elixir for skin, nails, and hair.

Habitat & Region: Thriving in damp environments, horsetail is typically found in wetlands.

Identification: Standing tall, horsetail is easily recognizable by its thick, segmented stature adorned with tiny fern-like protrusions. Its resemblance to a small bamboo is notable.

- **Stems:** The hollow, ribbed stems of horsetail not only make for efficient scrubbers but are also distinctively segmented.
- **Leaves:** Miniature in size, the leaves resemble ferns and emerge from horsetail's segments.

Medicinal Parts: The plant's green stems hold its medicinal prowess.

How to Harvest: Horsetail stems can be harvested throughout the year.

Making Medicine: Strong Horsetail Infusion and Tea:

- Combine ½ cup of horsetail with 2 cups of water.
- Bring to a boil and let simmer for 10 minutes.
- Remove from heat and allow the mixture to steep for an hour.

Dosage: The prepared infusion serves a myriad of purposes:

- **Hair Rinse:** Provides luster and strength to hair.
- **Skin Tonic:** Helps improve the skin's elasticity and reduce the appearance of fine lines.
- **Gargle:** Effective for alleviating sore throats and combating gingivitis.

WARNINGS:

- While horsetail has numerous benefits, it's important to use it with caution. Overconsumption can lead to potential side effects such as thiamine deficiency and diuretic issues.

- Always ensure you are identifying horsetail correctly. Other species, like the toxic "marsh horsetail" (Equisetum palustre), may look similar. Consumption of the wrong variety can be harmful.

- As with any herbal remedy, it is advisable to consult with a healthcare professional before incorporating it into your routine.

Hyssop (Hyssopus officinalis)

Plant Name: Hyssop

Plant Type: Long Blooming Perennial Herb

Lore: Often cited in religious texts, hyssop has a long-standing association with purification rituals. It is also a boon for pollinators, attracting bees, butterflies, and other beneficial insects with its vivid flowers.

What Does it Treat: Hyssop has traditionally been used for respiratory conditions, including coughs, asthma, and bronchitis. It's also been used for digestive issues like gas and colic. Additionally, it has astringent properties, making it useful for cuts and wounds.

Habitat & Region: Hyssop thrives in sunny locations with well-draining soil. It's often found in highland prairies and dry highland woods.

Identification: Hyssop is a robust plant growing between 2-4 feet tall, characterized by multiple stems showcasing spear-pointed leaves and a profusion of tubular flowers.

- **Flowers:** Tubular in shape and occurring in shades of blue, lavender, or purple, they make up a significant part of the stem.
- **Leaves:** Green and lanceolate, these veiny leaves are opposite and somewhat aromatic when crushed.

Medicinal Parts: The aerial parts (those above ground) of the hyssop plant are used for medicinal purposes.

How to Harvest: Using a sharp pair of shears, cut the hyssop, ensuring you take only the healthy parts of the plant.

Making Medicine:

- Hyssop Infusion and Tea: Use 2oz of hyssop in 1 cup of boiling water, let it steep for 15 minutes.

- Hyssop Poultice: Rehydrate dried hyssop or finely chop/process fresh hyssop. Apply the paste to the affected area, such as a cut or wound, before bandaging.

Dosage: For digestive discomforts, consume up to 3 cups of hyssop tea per day.

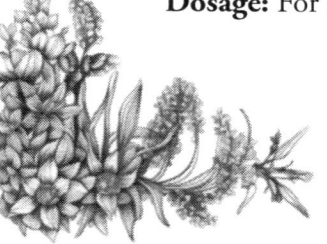

WARNINGS:

- Consuming hyssop oil or high doses can lead to seizures, so it's essential to use the herb in moderation.

- Pregnant or breastfeeding women should avoid consuming hyssop as its safety hasn't been thoroughly established for this group.

- As with many herbs, there can be interactions with medications, so it's crucial to consult with a healthcare professional before using hyssop therapeutically.

Jasmine (Jasminum officinale)

Plant Name: Jasmine

Plant Type: Subtropical climbing shrub

Lore: Revered for its enchanting aroma, jasmine has deep cultural roots. In the West, it's associated with love and romance, symbolizing Venus in Roman and Aphrodite in Greek mythology. In some Eastern cultures, jasmine flowers are a symbol of affection, purity, and grace.

What Does it Treat:

- **Anxiety Relief:** The calming scent of jasmine is known to have a relaxing effect on the mind and can help reduce feelings of stress and anxiety.

- **Pain Relief:** Jasmine has analgesic properties that can alleviate various types of pain, from muscular fatigue to earaches.

Habitat & Region: Prefers subtropical and tropical regions, where it can receive ample sunlight and rain.

Identification:

- **Flowers:** Long, thin, or sometimes shorter and rounded, but consistently white, often with a sweet, alluring fragrance.
- **Leaves:** Oval-shaped, leathery, and dark green, growing from tendrils branching off from the main vine.

Medicinal Parts: Both the aromatic flowers and the leaves are used for therapeutic purposes.

How to Harvest: Gently pluck the flower buds and leaves, or trim them using shears, preferably during early morning or late evening when the aromatic compounds are the most concentrated.

Making Medicine:

- Jasmine Oil: Fill a small mason jar with jasmine flowers and buds. Cover them with a carrier oil (like grapeseed or jojoba). Seal the jar and let it sit in a cool, dark place for a couple of weeks, allowing the jasmine essence to infuse the oil.

Dosage: The infused jasmine oil can be applied directly to the skin, added to bathwater, or even used as a massage oil. Its soothing aroma makes it perfect for aromatherapy.

WARNINGS:

- Always do a patch test when applying any new oil or product to your skin to ensure you're not allergic.

- While there might not be dangerous jasmine look-alikes, there are different varieties of jasmine. Not all types of jasmine are edible or safe for all uses. For instance, the yellow-flowering Jasminum fruticans is not the same as the white-flowering varieties used in teas or perfumes. Always ensure you have the correct variety for your intended use.

- Consuming large quantities of jasmine essential oil can be toxic. Always dilute essential oils and use them under guidance.

Jewelweed (Impatiens capensis)

Plant Name: Jewelweed (also known as Spotted Touch-Me-Not)

Plant Type: Flowering Herbaceous Perennial

Habitat & Region: Jewelweed thrives in wetlands, particularly near streams or in damp woods across North America.

Identification:

- **Flowers:** Distinctive in appearance, the trumpet-shaped flowers are usually a bright orange or yellow hue, adorned with small spots, giving a horn or cornucopia-like appearance.
- **Seed Pod:** The seed pods are spring-loaded and will "explode" when touched, dispersing their seeds. This characteristic gives the plant its nickname, "Touch-Me-Not."
- **Leaves:** Ovular with scalloped edges, the leaves are often slightly iridescent when submerged in water, which is one of the reasons it's named "Jewelweed."

Medicinal Parts: The leaves and stems of the plant are renowned for their ability to provide relief from the itchy rash caused by poison ivy and other skin irritations.

How to Harvest: The whole plant can be harvested using shears or by hand-pulling.

What Does it Treat:

- **Dermatitis:** Particularly the rash from poison ivy, oak, or sumac.

- **Fungal Infections:** Effective against athlete's foot.

Making Medicine:

- Salve: Blend jewelweed with a carrier oil (like coconut or olive oil) and optionally beeswax to create a thicker consistency. Heat gently until combined and pour into containers to cool.

- Poultice: Crush fresh leaves and stems and apply directly to the affected area.

Dosage: Apply the salve or poultice to the affected area as often as needed.

WARNINGS:

- Ingestion: Jewelweed should not be ingested as it can cause adverse reactions. Always use it topically.

- Skin Test: Before applying extensively, always test any herbal remedy on a small area of skin to ensure there's no allergic reaction.

Lavender (Lavandula angustifolia)

Plant Name: Lavender

Plant Type: Perennial Herb

Habitat & Region: Thrives in hilly meadows and rocky soils. Although native to the Mediterranean region, it has been cultivated worldwide.

Identification:

- **Flowers:** Lavender flowers are tubular, violet-blue to lavender in hue, and densely clustered on slender spikes. Their distinctive aroma makes them easily recognizable.
- **Leaves:** Opposite, oblong to linear, and range from green to gray-green. Unlike rosemary, they have a slightly fuzzy texture due to fine hairs.

Medicinal Parts: Flowers are the most commonly used, but stems and leaves also possess medicinal properties.

How to Harvest: Use kitchen shears to trim the stems, preferably during the morning after the dew has evaporated and just when the buds are about to open.

What Does it Treat:

- Mood & Nervous System: Lavender is known for its calming properties, helping to reduce anxiety, depression, and stress.

- Sleep Disorders: It can alleviate insomnia and improve sleep quality.

- Skin Conditions: Lavender possesses antiseptic and anti-inflammatory properties, making it useful for minor burns and bug bites.

- Hair Care: It can promote hair growth and treat conditions like dandruff.

Making Medicine:

- **Bath:** A few drops of lavender essential oil or a handful of dried flowers can be added to a hot bath for relaxation.

- **Tea:** Combine dried lavender flowers with other calming herbs like chamomile for a soothing infusion.

- **Salve:** Mix lavender-infused oil with beeswax to create a calming and healing salve.

- **Essential Oil:** Lavender essential oil is extracted through steam distillation and has concentrated benefits. It can be diluted with carrier oils for massage or added to diffusers for aromatherapy.

Dosage:

- **Tea:** 1-2 teaspoons of dried flowers steeped in hot water for 5-10 minutes, consumed once or twice daily.

- **Topical:** Lavender salves, creams, or diluted essential oil can be applied directly to the skin as needed.

WARNINGS:

- Allergy: Some individuals may be allergic to lavender; always conduct a patch test before extensive use.

- Pregnancy & Breastfeeding: While generally considered safe, it's recommended to consult a healthcare provider before using any herbal remedies during pregnancy or breastfeeding.

- Ingesting Essential Oil: Essential oils are potent, and ingesting them can be harmful. Ensure proper dilution and never consume them without expert advice.

Lemon Balm (Melissa officinalis)

Plant Name: Lemon Balm

Plant Type: Herbaceous Perennial Herb

Lore: An herb in the mint family, lemon balm has been utilized for its medicinal properties for centuries. With its soothing properties, it has been added to teas for relaxation and remedying stress.

What Does it Treat:

- **Mood & Nervous System:** Lemon balm is widely used to alleviate symptoms of anxiety, stress, and depression.

- **Sleep Disorders:** Its calming effect makes it ideal for combating insomnia.

- **Digestive System:** It provides relief from digestive discomforts such as bloating and gas.

Habitat & Region: Lemon balm is versatile and can thrive in various conditions. Ideally, it loves sunny prairies, but it can also grow in shady areas, sunny wetlands, and disturbed grounds.

Identification:

- **Flowers:** As summer progresses, lemon balm produces small white flowers.
- **Leaves:** The heart-shaped, serrated leaves are a clear indication of its belonging to the mint family. Rubbing them releases a distinct lemony scent.

Medicinal Parts: Primarily the leaves are used for therapeutic purposes.

How to Harvest: Utilize kitchen shears to snip the stalks as desired.

Making Medicine:

- **Tea:** Lemon balm leaves can be steeped to make a calming tea. Use 2oz per cup and steep for 10 minutes.

- **Tincture:** A lemon balm tincture can be made using a 1:5 ratio with 30% alcohol. This offers a concentrated dosage of its benefits.

- **Salve:** Due to its soothing properties, it can be infused in oils to create a comforting salve.

Dosage:

- Tea: Sip 2-3 cups of lemon balm tea daily for relaxation.

- Tincture: 2 dropperfuls twice daily can provide concentrated benefits.

WARNINGS:

Identification: Always ensure that you're harvesting the correct plant. The distinctive lemon scent of lemon balm leaves is a key identifier. If you don't detect it upon rubbing the leaves, you might be dealing with a different plant from the mint family or another herb altogether.

Licorice Root (Glycyrrhiza glabra)

Plant Name: Licorice Root

Plant Type: Perennial Herb

Lore: Licorice root has been historically used not just for its medicinal qualities but also as a natural oral care tool. Its fibrous texture allows it to be chewed and used as a makeshift toothbrush.

What Does it Treat:

- Digestive System: Licorice root is renowned for alleviating various gastrointestinal disturbances including acid reflux, heartburn, and stomach ulcers.

Habitat & Region: Licorice prefers full sun and well-draining soil. It doesn't thrive under heavy canopies and avoids overly saturated soils.

Identification:

- **Flowers:** Bluish-purple flowers make a striking appearance along the stalks in the summer.
- **Leaves:** The plant features green oval, lancelet leaves.
- **Roots:** Recognizable for its distinctive licorice aroma, the root is flexible, with a yellow inner core.

Medicinal Parts: The primary medicinal part of this plant is the root.

How to Harvest: A gardening fork or spade is the best tool to extract licorice roots from the ground.

Making Medicine:

- **Decoction:** For a hot decoction, use 1 tablespoon of licorice root per cup of water. Simmer for 10 minutes and strain before drinking.

- **Tincture:** A tincture can be made using a 1:5 ratio with 50% alcohol, allowing for a potent extract of the root's benefits.

Dosage:

- Decoction: Drink 2-3 cups daily as required.

- Tincture: Two dropperfuls per day is the recommended dose.

WARNINGS (high dose dangerous, dangerous lookalikes)

- Overconsumption: Chronic consumption of licorice can lead to side effects like high blood pressure, potassium deficiency, and edema. It is crucial to use licorice root as a temporary remedy rather than a long-term solution.

- Medication Interference: Licorice root can also interfere with certain medications. It's always wise to consult with a healthcare professional before introducing any herbal remedies, especially if you're on medication or have underlying health conditions.

Lotus (Nelumbo nucifera)

Plant Name: Lotus

Plant Type: Rhizomatous Water Plant

Lore: Revered in many ancient cultures, particularly in Chinese medicine, the lotus has been utilized for its medicinal properties for over a millennium.

What Does it Treat:

- **Digestive Issues:** The root of the lotus plant, known for its unique appearance and nutritional benefits, has been used to remedy intestinal infections and diarrhea.
- **Mental Health:** Seeds and flowers are believed to alleviate symptoms of anxiety.
- **Nutritional Value:** Lotus is a good source of nutrition, providing several essential vitamins and minerals.

Habitat & Region: Preferring still or slow-moving waters, the lotus thrives in ponds and lakes.

Identification:

- **Flowers:** Known for their elegance, lotus flowers come in a variety of hues including pink, purple, and white. Their structure – particularly their distinct petals – differentiates them from other aquatic blooms.
- **Leaves:** Floating atop the water's surface, the large, round green leaves of the lotus are often referred to as "lily pads".
- **Roots:** These starchy tubers, which are both edible and medicinal, have a unique appearance: somewhat resembling a chain of sausages, with holes running through their centers.

Medicinal Parts: The lotus is versatile in its benefits. Every part of the plant, from its roots to its seeds, holds medicinal and nutritional value.

How to Harvest: Equipped with appropriate gear like waders or waterproof boots, one can harvest the lotus by extracting it, roots and all, from the base of the water body it inhabits.

Making Medicine:

- **Infusion:** For a lotus root tea, combine half an ounce of the root with a quart of water and simmer for 10 minutes.

- **Seeds:** The seeds can be roasted and consumed, providing a range of health benefits.

Dosage: The lotus root tea can be consumed 2-3 times a day.

WARNINGS: While the lotus is beneficial, it's crucial to distinguish it from its lookalike: the water lily. Water lilies are toxic when ingested. A key differentiator is the flower's structure. Water lilies have sharp, dagger-like petals, symbolizing danger, while lotus petals are more curved, rounded, and pointed. Always ensure proper identification before consumption.

Maple Tree (Acer sp.)

Plant Name: Maple Tree

Plant Type: Deciduous Tree

Lore: Iconically recognized as Canada's national emblem, the maple leaf graces the nation's flag and has a rich history tied to the land.

What Does it Treat:

- **Detoxification:** The leaves and bark of the maple tree have been traditionally used to support the body's natural detoxification systems, especially the liver and gallbladder.

- **Sedative:** Maple leaf tea can also serve as a mild sedative, helping to calm nerves and promote relaxation.

Habitat & Region: Maples thrive in a variety of regions, from forests to urban landscapes, largely in the northern hemisphere, especially in Canada and parts of the US.

Identification:

- **Flowers:** Maple trees produce long tubular flowers that are typically red, with small, delicate petals.
- **Leaves:** Perhaps the most identifiable feature, maple leaves typically have 3-5 lobes, with serrated edges. The exact shape and color can vary depending on the specific species.
- **Bark:** : The bark of mature maple trees is characterized by its long, fine, and scaly grey plates.

Medicinal Parts: The leaves are the primary medicinal part of the maple tree, but the bark also holds value.

How to Harvest: Leaves can be easily plucked from branches. If harvesting bark, ensure you're using a sharp knife and only take what you need, being careful not to harm the tree excessively.

Making Medicine:

- **Maple Tea:** Steep 1 teaspoon of dried leaves or bark in 1 cup of boiling water for about 10 minutes.

Dosage: Consume the maple tea 2-3 times daily, preferably between meals.

WARNINGS:

- **Lookalikes:** There are several trees whose leaves may resemble those of the maple, but a distinguishing feature of maple trees is their paired opposite leaf arrangement. Always ensure accurate identification before use.

- **Overconsumption:** As with all herbal remedies, moderation is key. Overconsumption of maple leaf tea can potentially cause adverse effects, so always stick to recommended dosages.

Mallow (Malva sylvestris)

Plant Name: Mallow

Plant Type: Annual or biennial weed

Lore: Historically, sap extracted from the mallow root was utilized in the creation of the original marshmallow confectionery.

What Does it Treat:

- **Inflammation:** The mucilaginous nature of mallow root makes it an effective remedy for inflammation, particularly within the digestive and urinary tracts.

- **Respiratory:** It also acts as a soothing agent for coughs stemming from lung inflammation.

Habitat & Region: Mallow thrives in domestic settings such as gardens and yards. Though often dismissed as a mere weed, it boasts potent medicinal properties.

Identification:

- **Appearance:** Mallow is a low-growing plant with lightly fuzzy stems originating from a deep taproot. It features leathery, glossy leaves.
- **Flowers:** Its flowers are small and white, with five petals surrounding a rounded white center.
- **Leaves:** Seven-sided, serrated, and pointy, mallow leaves have a distinct appearance.
- **Roots:** Mallow's root is reminiscent of licorice root in appearance—long, slender, and encased in thin skin.

Medicinal Parts: The root of the mallow plant is the primary medicinal component.

How to Harvest: Using a hand shovel, carefully dig around the root to loosen the soil. Once loosened, gently pull the root from the ground.

Making Medicine:
- **Mallow Root Infusion:**
  - Slice the mallow root into smaller pieces.
  - Fill a mason jar about a quarter of the way with the slices (a couple of roots might be needed).
  - Pour warm water into the jar, covering the root, and seal with a lid.

- Allow the mixture to sit for a minimum of four hours, though leaving it overnight is optimal.
- Once infused, strain the roots to obtain a slightly viscous liquid. Ensure you label the jar to avoid confusion.

Dosage: For alleviating inflammation, heartburn, or coughs, consume a few tablespoons of the mallow infusion.

WARNINGS:

- **Allergic Reactions:** As with all herbs, it's possible for some individuals to experience allergic reactions. It's essential to ensure you aren't allergic to mallow before consuming in any form.
- **Lookalikes:** While mallow is distinct in its features, there are other plants that might superficially resemble it. Always ensure accurate identification before consumption.
- **Pregnancy and Breastfeeding:** Pregnant or breastfeeding women should consult with a healthcare professional before consuming mallow or any other medicinal herb.

Milk Thistle (Silybum marianum)

Plant Name: Milk Thistle

Plant Type: Thick Stalked Distinct Biennial or Annual Plant

Lore: With a rich history spanning over two millennia, milk thistle has served both culinary and medicinal purposes.

What Does it Treat:

- **Appetite Stimulant:** Helps increase the desire to eat.

- **Digestive Aid:** Assists in breaking down food.

- **Liver Health:** Acts as a tonic, renowned for detoxifying and protecting the liver.

- **Gallbladder Health:** Supports and cleanses the gallbladder.

- **Poisoning Treatment:** Historically, it's been used to counteract the effects of mushroom poisoning.

Habitat & Region: Prefers sun-drenched, rocky terrains and thrives in arid conditions. It's also found in areas neglected by cultivation.

Identification:

- **Appearance:** Recognizable by its menacing spikes.
- **Flowers:** The flower head is the plant's standout feature, showcasing hues ranging from light purple to pink. The petals ascend from a green, bulbous base, which is framed by thorny sepals.
- **Leaves:** Sporting lance-like structures, the leaves bear white veins. Over time, the leafy spikes become increasingly sharp.
- **Stem:** Its stems might be bristly or even thorny, demanding caution during handling.

Medicinal Parts: The seeds of the milk thistle are primarily harnessed for their healing properties.

How to Harvest: As flower heads wane and dry, harvest them and let them further desiccate in a paper bag for around a week. One mature flower head can yield approximately 200 seeds.

Making Medicine:

- **Milk Thistle Tea:** For preparation, bring a cup of water to a boil. Add 2 teaspoons of milk thistle seeds to the boiling water. Allow the concoction to steep for about 5 minutes before straining.

Dosage: For therapeutic effects, consume 2-3 cups of milk thistle tea daily.

WARNINGS:

- Overconsumption: Taking excessive amounts of milk thistle can lead to stomach upsets.

- Allergic Reactions: Some might be allergic to components of milk thistle. Initial, minimal intake is advisable to check for adverse reactions.

- Drug Interactions: Milk thistle might interact with certain medications. Always consult a healthcare professional before incorporating it into your regimen.

- Lookalikes: While milk thistle is distinctive, there might be other thorny plants that resemble it. Proper identification is crucial to avoid ingesting potentially harmful plants.

Mint (Mentha sp.)

Plant Name: Mint

Plant Type: Perennial Herb

Habitat & Region: Often found in moist meadows and wetlands, mint thrives in conditions with good moisture.

Identification: This popular culinary herb is easily identifiable through its distinctive aroma and appearance.

- **Flowers:** Mint showcases a spire of petite, clustered flowers in hues of pink to purple.
- **Leaves:** Mint leaves are wrinkled in texture and grow abundantly along the stems. They exude a potent minty aroma when crushed or rubbed.

Medicinal Parts: Both the leaves and stems are beneficial. Essentially, the entire above-ground part of the plant can be harvested for medicinal purposes.

How to Harvest: Lightweight pruners or shears work well to clip the mint stems.

What Does it Treat:
- **Topical Relief:** Mint oil or salve provides solace to weary hands and feet. When applied to the temples, it can alleviate moderate headaches.
- **Digestive Aid:** Consumed internally, mint supports digestion and addresses issues like high stomach acid or indigestion.

1. Mint Tea (Infusion):
- **Ingredients:** Fresh or dried mint leaves, boiling water.
- **Preparation:**
  - Place a handful of fresh or 1-2 teaspoons of dried mint leaves in a cup.
  - Pour boiling water over the leaves.
  - Cover and steep for 10-15 minutes.
  - Strain out the leaves and drink.

Dosage: While mint is generally safe, a minority might experience adverse effects like nausea or skin irritation. If your initial experience is positive, you can freely consume or apply mint. However, always begin with smaller doses to ensure no adverse reactions.

WARNINGS:

- **Verification:** The strong minty scent of this herb makes it relatively easy to confirm its identity, reducing the risk of mistaking it for other plants.

- **Pregnancy:** High doses during pregnancy might not be advisable. Always consult with a healthcare provider before using any herbal remedies during pregnancy.

- **Drug Interaction:** Mint may affect the way certain medications work, so always consult with a doctor before mixing medications and herbal remedies.

Motherwort (Leonurus cardiaca)

Plant Name: Motherwort

Plant Type: Herbaceous Perennial

Lore: Rooted in Japanese folklore, tales recount of a village whose residents drank from a stream flowing through motherwort fields, allegedly bestowing upon them lifespans extending up to 130 years.

What Does it Treat:

- **Heart Support:** Historically employed for heart conditions and palpitations.

- **Women's Health:** Beneficial for menstrual discomfort and menopausal symptoms.

- **Anxiety and Stress:** Traditionally utilized for its calming attributes.

- **Thyroid Function:** Known to support those with certain thyroid conditions.

Habitat & Region: Often found in areas such as neglected gardens, meadows, and field edges.

Identification:

- **Appearance:** Sturdy stem supporting an array of flowers and leaves.
- **Flowers:** From July to September, these flowers can vary from pale pink to purple, with a unique thistle-like appearance underneath.
- **Leaves:** Beginning as broad and tri-lobed, as they ascend the stem, they develop into a five-lobed form, the central lobe being most prominent.

Medicinal Parts: The leaves, flowers, and stems are preferred for their medicinal properties.

How to Harvest: Wear gloves due to the potential risk of dermatitis. Ideal for harvesting are young shoots, leaves, and flowers.

Making Medicine:

- **Motherwort Tincture:** Fill a mason jar half full with motherwort, then top off with apple cider vinegar or a 100-proof alcohol. Seal and keep in a dark location for roughly 6 weeks. After infusion, strain out the plant matter.

Dosage: Recommended daily intake ranges from 10-20 drops of the tincture.

WARNINGS:

- **Digestive Problems:** Consuming in excess may cause gastrointestinal issues, including cramps and diarrhea.

- **Blood Thinning:** Might influence blood clotting. If on blood thinners or anticipating surgery, consult with a medical professional.

Mugwort (Artemisia vulgaris)

Plant Name: Mugwort

Plant Type: Aromatic Perennial Herb

Lore: Mugwort, scientifically known as Artemisia vulgaris, derives its name from the lunar goddess Artemis, symbolizing its ancient association with moon rituals and women's health.

What Does it Treat:

- **Women's Health:** Historically used to induce childbirth and regulate menstruation.
- **Digestive Aid:** Known to stimulate appetite and counteract nausea.

Habitat & Region: Thrives in fields and waste areas, often seen on disturbed grounds.

Identification:

- **Appearance:** Mugwort stands out with its reddish or greenish-yellow disk-shaped flowers and pungent scent. Typically, its stems grow to about 3 feet.
- **Flowers:** These are small and are grouped in panicles, budding off longer stems that trail up the plant.
- **Leaves:** Deeply lobed, pointed, and sectional, the leaves of mugwort might remind one of an enlarged version of flat-leaf parsley.

Medicinal Parts: Predominantly, the flowers of mugwort are harvested for medicinal use.

How to Harvest: Wait for the flowers to dry on the plant. Harvesting them is akin to stripping rosemary or thyme leaves from their stems - it can be done by pinching the base of the flower and pulling upwards.

Making Medicine:

- **Mugwort Tincture:** Start by filling a 12oz mason jar halfway with dried mugwort flowers. Top it up with vodka until the jar is full. Seal it and store in a dark and cool place, like a pantry or cabinet, for 6 weeks to allow for maceration. After this period, strain out the plant material.

Dosage: A typical dose of the mugwort tincture is 20-40 drops before meals.

WARNINGS:

- **Overconsumption:** High doses of mugwort can lead to symptoms like restlessness, insomnia, or even hallucinations.

- **Pregnancy:** Given its historical use to induce childbirth, pregnant women should avoid mugwort as it may stimulate uterine contractions.

- **Allergies:** Mugwort pollen might cause allergic reactions in some individuals.

- **Lookalikes:** While mugwort is distinct, it's crucial to correctly identify it. Some plants, like wormwood or chrysanthemum, might have a superficial resemblance to mugwort. Always ensure you're harvesting the correct plant.

Mullein (Verbascum thapsus)

Plant Name: Mullein (Verbascum thapsus)

Plant Type: Herbaceous Perennial

Habitat & Region: Mullein thrives in a variety of habitats including creek banks, roadsides, and disturbed grounds. Its adaptability also allows it to grow on the fringes of forests.

Identification:

- **General:** Starting as a modest rosette, mullein transforms into a towering plant as summer progresses. It's most recognizable feature is a tall stalk, potentially reaching up to 6 feet, adorned with vibrant yellow flowers.
- **Flowers:** Each petite yellow flower has five petals. The sheer number of these flowers clustering up the stalk makes mullein unmistakable in its habitat.
- **Leaves:** A basal rosette of large, fuzzy leaves surrounds the base of the plant. Their soft and hairy texture is another distinct identifying feature.

Medicinal Parts: Primarily, the leaves and flowers are harvested for their therapeutic properties.

How to Harvest: The leaves and flowers can be gently plucked by hand, or for a more efficient harvest, garden shears or scissors can be used.

What Does it Treat:

- **Respiratory Aid:** Mullein is celebrated in herbal medicine for its efficacy in treating upper respiratory conditions, including asthma, bronchitis, and cold symptoms.

- **Soothing Properties:** Its emollient nature can also help soothe irritated membranes.

Making Medicine:

- **Hot Infusion (Tea):** Mullein leaves or flowers can be steeped in boiling water for 10-15 minutes. Strain before drinking to avoid any fine hairs from the plant.

- **Tincture:** The leaves and flowers can be macerated in alcohol to create a tincture, which should be stored in a dark place for several weeks before straining.

Dosage:

- **Tea:** Consume 1 cup of the mullein infusion three times daily.

- **Tincture:** Administer 5ml of the tincture 2-3 times daily.

WARNINGS:

- **Unique Identification:** Mullein is a uniquely tall and distinct plant, with no known plants that closely resemble it in appearance.

- **Fine Hairs:** When consumed, the tiny hairs from the leaves might cause throat irritation. Ensure any infusions are well-strained before consumption.

- **Interactions:** Always consult a healthcare professional before introducing a new herbal remedy to ensure there are no adverse interactions with existing medications or conditions.

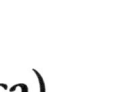

Nettle, Stinging (Urtica dioica)

Plant Name: Stinging Nettle

Plant Type: Large Rhizomatous Perennial

Habitat & Region: Found predominantly in wetlands and moist environments.

Identification:

- **General:** Stinging nettle, true to its name, is notorious for the tiny hair-like structures (trichomes) covering its stem and leaves. These trichomes contain formic acid, which, upon contact, can cause an itchy rash, commonly known as the "7-minute itch." However, the irritant property of these trichomes is nullified when the plant is dried or cooked.
- **Flowers:** The plant sports green catkins that cluster along its stem.
- **Leaves:** The leaves have a slightly fuzzy appearance due to the presence of numerous trichomes.

Medicinal Parts: The entire plant can be used for medicine.

Medicinal Parts: Every part of the stinging nettle, from root to tip, possesses medicinal qualities.

How to Harvest: Extreme caution is imperative during the harvesting process. It's essential to wear gloves to protect your skin from the stinging trichomes. Mature plants, with their thicker stalks, might require the use of pruners for efficient harvesting.

What Does it Treat:

- **Anti-inflammatory:** Can alleviate muscle and joint pain.
- **Skin Ailments:** Known to be effective against eczema.
- **Joint Conditions:** Can provide relief from arthritis and gout symptoms.
- **Blood Health:** A potential treatment for anemia.

Making Medicine:

- **Hot Infusion/Tea:** Use 1 oz of nettle leaf to 1 cup of hot water.
- **Tincture (Leaf):** 1:2 ratio using 50% or higher alcohol concentration.
- **Decoction (Root):** Boiling nettle root in water until its medicinal properties are extracted.

- **Tincture (Root):** 1:5 ratio using 30% alcohol.

Dosage:

- **Hot Infusion/Tea:** Consume 2-3 times daily.

- **Tincture:** Administer 2 mL, three times a day.

WARNINGS:

- **Immediate Skin Reaction:** Direct contact with the fresh plant can result in skin irritation due to its stinging hairs. Always handle with gloves.

- **Lookalikes:** While stinging nettle is quite distinct, some plants might be mistaken for it. It's crucial to be well-acquainted with its features for safe harvesting and usage.

- **Potential Overconsumption:** Excessive intake might lead to stomach upset or other side effects. Always use medicinal plants under the guidance of a healthcare professional.

Oregano (Origanum vulgare)

Plant Name: Oregano

Plant Type: Perennial Culinary Herb

Habitat & Region: Thrives in dry prairie regions and well-drained soils.

Identification:

- **General:** Oregano, recognized for its woody stems and small, fuzzy leaves, emits a distinctive fragrance which aids in its identification. The plant usually reaches a height of about 2 feet when fully grown.
- **Flowers:** The oregano plant bears small, pinkish-purple flowers that are characterized by their prominent stamens..
- **Leaves:** These are petite in size and resemble a rounded arrowhead in shape.

Medicinal Parts: The entire aerial part (everything above the ground) of the oregano plant has medicinal attributes.

How to Harvest: Using kitchen shears, snip the desired parts gently.

What Does it Treat:

- **Respiratory Ailments:** Effective against flu and common cold symptoms.
- **Digestive Upsets:** Can alleviate stomach discomforts.
- **Menstrual Pain:** Assists in alleviating menstrual cramps and pain.
- **Fever:** Can aid in reducing mild fever.

Making Medicine:

- **Hot Infusion/Tea:** For this preparation, use 2 oz of oregano per cup of hot water.
- **Tincture:** Opt for a 1:2 ratio, employing 50% alcohol.

Dosage:

- **Hot Infusion/Tea: Recommended intake is up to 3 cups daily.**
- **Tincture: Administer 2 dropperfuls once a day.**

WARNINGS:

- **Pregnancy:** Medicinal preparations of oregano should be avoided by pregnant women.

- **Overconsumption:** Oregano, when consumed in excessive quantities, can have adverse effects. Always adhere to recommended dosages and consult with a healthcare professional before starting any herbal remedy.

- **Lookalikes:** While oregano is quite distinct, especially due to its fragrance, it's crucial to ensure proper identification to avoid potential confusion with other plants.

Passionflower (Passiflora)

Plant Type: Perennial Wildflower

Lore: The passionflower's fruit is commonly referred to as the "maypop". This moniker originates from the pastime of children jumping on the fruit to delight in the distinctive "pop" sound it would produce.

What Does it Treat:

- **Nervous Tension:** Functions as a mild nerve sedative.

- **Sleeplessness:** Acts as a sleep aid to promote restfulness.

Habitat & Region: Passionflower can often be found flourishing along fence lines, field edges, and around fences.

Identification:

- **General:** Passionflower is a unique climbing plant, employing tendrils for support and mobility. It is renowned for its striking flowers and yields a delectable fruit encased in a green hull, which reveals a flavorful, seeded core when opened.
- **Flowers:** The flowers are captivating, varying from brilliant white to blue shades. They feature pronounced stamens and are surrounded by an array of slender, elongated petals.
- **Leaves:** These are relatively mundane in comparison to the flower, presenting as spear-shaped and green with gentle serrations.

Medicinal Parts:

- **Above Ground:** The aerial parts of the plant can produce a calming, sedative effect.

- **Root:** Historically, the Cherokee Indians utilized the root of the passionflower for the alleviation of earaches and to treat wounds caused by thorns.

How to Harvest:

- **Above Ground:** Using shears, carefully trim the desired parts.

- **Roots:** A hori hori knife can be useful in extracting the roots.

Making Medicine:

- **Hot Infusion/Tea:** Combine 2 oz of passionflower (leaves and flowers) with 1 cup of hot water. Allow the mixture to steep for 10 minutes.

Dosage:

For best results, consume one cup of the infusion or tea as a relaxing nightcap to aid sleep.

WARNINGS:

- **Overconsumption:** Consuming excessive amounts of passionflower can lead to adverse effects, such as dizziness or gastrointestinal issues.
- **Lookalikes:** While passionflower is fairly distinct, always ensure accurate identification to prevent confusion with other plants. Before beginning any herbal treatment, consultation with a healthcare professional is advised.

Pine Tree (Pinus sp.)

Plant Name: Pine Tree

Plant Type: Evergreen Tree

Habitat & Region: The pine tree is commonly found in mixed forests and evergreen forests.

Identification:

- **General:** The Eastern white pine is the prime choice for medicinal uses. These trees can grow between 50 and 80 feet tall and can be recognized by their long green needles and pinecones.
- **Flowers:** Pine trees feature small, yellowish, knob-like flowers that eventually develop into cones.
- **Leaves:** The leaves of the pine tree are its identifiable long green needles.
- **Bark:** The bark is deeply furrowed, exhibiting a reddish-brown hue.

Medicinal Parts: The medicinal component of the pine tree is primarily its needles.

How to Harvest:

- **Fallen Branches:** Often, fallen branches will still retain some needles which can be harvested.

- **Directly from the Tree:** If harvesting directly from a tree, you can either pull the needles off or use pruners for a cleaner cut.

What Does it Treat:

- **Immune System: Pine needle tea is known to boost immunity.**

- **Vitamin Source: It's a rich source of Vitamin C, providing approximately 250mg per cup.**

Making Medicine:

- To make a pine needle tea, bring two cups of water to a boil. Once boiled, remove from heat and add a generous handful of pine needles. Allow the mixture to steep for about 20 minutes. For added flavor and benefits, a slice of lemon can be introduced to the tea.

Dosage:

- It's recommended to consume 3-4 cups of pine needle tea per day.

WARNINGS:

Yew Tree: One must be vigilant to avoid confusing pine trees with yew trees. Yew trees have flat needles and produce a distinctive red fruit that appears as though it's been pitted. It is important to note that yew trees are toxic. The red fruit and flat needles are clear indicators that differentiate yew trees from pines. Always make sure you are harvesting from a genuine pine tree to prevent accidental ingestion of toxic substances.

Common Plantain (Plantago lanceolata)

Plant Name: Common Plantain

Plant Type: Low Lying Broadleaf Perennial Plant

Lore: Hailing from the old world, this plant was introduced to Native Americans by European settlers. The Native Americans aptly nicknamed it "white man's foot," observing its rapid spread wherever Europeans tread.

What Does it Treat:

- **Wounds:** The primary medicinal application of common plantain is its potent wound-healing capacity when applied as a poultice.

Habitat & Region: Ubiquitous in nature, common plantain is likely to be spotted in your front yard, local park, and virtually anywhere with soil and sun.

Identification:

- **General Appearance:** A ground-hugging plant with oval-shaped leaves, it tends to grow in a rosette pattern. With time, it sends up a slender, leafless stalk crowned with a spiky flower.
- **Flowers:** Spiky in nature, these flowers emerge from a pencil-thin, solitary stalk that sprouts from the plant's center.
- **Leaves:** Characterized by their ovate shape.

Medicinal Parts: The leaf is the treasure trove of plantain's medicinal properties.

How to Harvest:

- **Tools:** Equipped with shears, one can easily snip off the leaves. When collecting in bulk, a colander or a breathable bag, such as burlap, proves handy.

Making Medicine: Given plantain's abundance, it's recommended to concoct both a salve and a poultice for versatile application.

- Poultice: Creating a poultice is straightforward. Simply grind the leaves using a mortar and pestle or mash them in a bowl. Alternatively, you can chew them and then apply the paste directly to cleaned wounds, securing with a bandage.

- Salve: Enhance the poultice by blending it with warmed beeswax. Not only does this ease the application, but the wax also forms a protective seal over the wound, shielding it from external contaminants.

Dosage: Reapply the poultice or salve to the wound during each dressing change.

WARNINGS:

- **Misidentification:** The ubiquity of common plantain makes it an easily recognizable plant, reducing the risks of confusing it with a harmful counterpart. Nonetheless, always ensure you've identified it correctly before use.

Queen Anne's Lace (Daucus carota)

Plant Name: Queen Anne's Lace

Plant Type: Wild Carrot

Lore: An intriguing kin, Silphium, from the same family, was once cherished for its contraceptive properties. Its demand was so immense that it became extinct around the 2nd or 3rd century.

What Does it Treat:

- **Digestive Issues:** Provides relief from indigestion and stomach upset.
- **Infertility:** Historically, it was believed to aid with fertility concerns.

Habitat & Region: Thriving in Fields and Meadows.

Identification:

- **General Appearance:** Named for its delicate lacy flowers, Queen Anne's Lace is recognizable by its intricate bloom.
- **Flowers:** These are clusters of small white flowers that come to bloom from late spring to early fall. Occasionally, a solitary purple flower can be seen at the center.
- **Leaves:** Highly reminiscent of parsley, these leaves are petite and feathery. But be cautious: they bear a striking similarity to the toxic poison hemlock.
- **Roots:** Looking and smelling like carrots, the roots are finger-thick and pale.

Medicinal Parts: The primary medicinal components are the seeds and the roots.

How to Harvest:

- **Tools:** Depending on the soil's compactness, either employ a small shovel or simply pull them out by hand.

Making Medicine:

- **Decoction:** Use either seeds or roots. For both, combine 4 tablespoons of the medicinal part with 4 cups of water. Bring the mixture to a simmer for 20 minutes.

Dosage:

- **Intake:** Consume ¼ cup of the decoction every 8 hours.

WARNINGS:

- **Dangerous Lookalikes:** Exercising caution is crucial when identifying Queen Anne's Lace. It closely mimics the appearance of poison hemlock, water hemlock, and fool's parsley. Consuming any of these toxic plants can be lethal. Always ensure proper identification before harvesting and consuming.

Rose (Rosa sp.)

Plant Name: Rose

Plant Type: Woody Flowering Perennial

Lore: Renowned for its unparalleled beauty and aroma, the rose has graced numerous civilizations, tracing back to the days of Mesopotamia under King Nebuchadnezzar. It was cultivated in ancient China, possibly as early as 5000 years ago. Ancient Egyptians buried rose wreaths in their tombs, while Greek myths narrate the divine origin of the rose.

What Does it Treat:

- Calming & Cooling: The rose is known for its soothing and cooling properties.
- Immunity Boost: Its rose hips are high in Vitamin C, making it an excellent choice for strengthening immunity.

Habitat & Region: Its extensive cultivation and travel history mean you can spot roses almost anywhere. They have a penchant for sun-soaked warm summers. They can occasionally be seen on the banks of large lakes and even occasionally in open fields.

Identification:

- **General Appearance:** The easily recognizable rose is known for its elegant flowers and thorny, woody stems.
- **Flowers:** Multi-petaled and available in various hues, roses are unmistakable.
- **Leaves:** Rose leaves are small, serrated, oval, and end in a point.
- **Hips:** Rose hips develop post the shedding of the flower petals and are best consumed post the season's first frost.

Medicinal Parts: Both the flower petals and the rose hips can be utilized.

How to Harvest:

- **Flower Petals:** Snip the entire flower off the stem and hang it in an upside-down position for drying.
- **Rose Hips:** Wait for the flower petals to naturally shed. Once they do, you can easily pick the rose hips by hand.

Making Medicine:

- Rose Petal Tea: Use 2 oz of rose petals per cup of water, steeping for about 10 minutes.

- Rose Hips: These can be eaten directly as a rich source of Vitamin C, benefiting the immune system.

Dosage:

- Restrict rose petal tea intake to 2-3 cups daily.

WARNINGS:

- **Identification:** Given its widespread familiarity, the rose is difficult to misidentify. The presence of thorns is a clear indication of its authenticity. However, always ensure you're harvesting from non-treated or non-pesticide sprayed plants.

Rosemary (Rosmarinus officinalis)

Plant Name: Rosemary

Plant Type: Perennial Evergreen Shrub

Lore: In Christian tradition, rosemary is believed to grow for 33 years, reaching the height of Jesus Christ when he was crucified, and then stops growing. It was burned to drive away evil spirits. According to another folklore, a man indifferent to the fragrance of rosemary could not offer true love to a woman.

What Does it Treat:

- Comprehensive Benefits: Rosemary is versatile. It boosts immunity, promotes brain health, detoxifies the liver, regulates hormones, and improves circulation when its oil is applied to the body. Additionally, it benefits the eyes, gums, skin, and hair and has anti-inflammatory properties.

Habitat & Region: Originally from the Mediterranean forests or scrublands, rosemary is now also seen growing solitarily in similar terrains in America.

Identification: The shrub's woody stalks and spruce-like leaves are distinctive, but it's the powerful scent that often confirms its identity.

- **Flowers:** Small and lavender-colored, rosemary flowers have an unusual appearance with long protruding stamens.
- **Leaves:** Resembling spruce needles, these leaves lack individual stems and emerge straight from the plant's stalk.

Medicinal Parts: Primarily the woody stems and the leaves.

How to Harvest: Use shears or pruners to snip the woody stems of the rosemary.

Making Medicine: Rosemary is adaptable and works well in various preparations like infused oils, decoctions, tinctures, salves, infusions, and fomentations.

- **Rosemary Hot Infusion:** Mix 2 oz of rosemary with 1 cup of water and steep for about 10 minutes.
- **Rosemary Infused Oil:** Pack several rosemary sprigs into a mason jar. Pour a high-quality carrier oil over it – while olive oil can be used, a neutral oil like grapeseed may be preferable as it

doesn't get affected as much by sunlight. Place the jar in a sunny window for several weeks. Post this, strain out the rosemary and store the oil in a cool, dark place.

Dosage:

- Consume 1-3 cups of the rosemary tea daily. Use the oil as needed.

WARNINGS:

- **Identification:** Rosemary's unique appearance and aroma make it difficult to misidentify.

- **Caution:** Very high doses of rosemary should be avoided. Pregnant women should refrain from using rosemary in medicinal quantities.

Sage (Salvia officinalis)

Plant Name: Sage

Plant Type: Perennial Herb

Lore: In the days of Ancient Egypt, sage was esteemed as a herb that could promote fertility.

What Does it Treat:

- Multifaceted Benefits: Sage is a versatile herb known to address various health concerns. Particularly, it's beneficial for oral health, aiding in treating mouth and gum issues. It also offers relief from respiratory problems and possesses anti-inflammatory properties that help reduce fever.

Habitat & Region: Sage has a preference for highland and rocky terrains, thriving under abundant sunshine. It also has a liking for shallow, not too moist, soil conditions.

Identification: One can recognize sage by its distinctively aromatic, large, and fuzzy oval leaves.

- **Flowers:** These are purple and bell-shaped, blossoming on a taller stem that stands out from the plant's leafy base.
- **Leaves:** The hallmark of sage, these leaves are textured and fuzzy. Depending on the variant, they can be broad and oval or slender and elongated.

Medicinal Parts: Primarily, it's the sage leaves that are sought after for their medicinal properties.

How to Harvest: Given the tender nature of sage leaves, they can be easily plucked by hand or snipped using shears.

Making Medicine:

- Sage Tincture: To prepare a sage tincture, take a mason jar and add roughly three handfuls of fresh sage leaves. Subsequently, fill the jar with 80 proof vodka. Seal the jar and remember to shake it from time to time. After a fortnight, your tincture is ready for use.

Dosage:

For the tincture, a quarter teaspoon taken thrice a day is the recommended dosage.

WARNINGS:

- Safety Concerns: It's imperative to exercise caution with sage intake as consuming it in extremely high quantities can lead to seizures.

- Distinct Identification: Given sage's unique characteristics, it's relatively easy to identify. However, always ensure you've correctly identified a plant before consumption.

Saint John's Wort (Hypericum perforatum)

Plant Name: Saint John's Wort

Plant Type: Herbaceous Perennial

Lore: St. John's Wort earned its name from its blooming season, which coincides with the feast of St. John the Baptist in late June. Historically, this herb has been used as a remedy for mental disorders for centuries.

What Does it Treat:

- Mental Health: Effective against Depression, Anxiety, and Seasonal Affective Disorder.
- Sleep Issues: Helps in addressing sleeping disorders.

Habitat & Region: You'll find it thriving along roadsides, in pastures, and open fields.

Identification: This herb grows almost everywhere around the world and is identified by its elongated, spotted leaves on a 3ft tall stalk.

- **Flowers:** The plant boasts small, bright yellow flowers with pointed petals that gather at the stalk's end.
- **Leaves:** These are stalkless and stand opposite each other. Their distinct feature is the lightly transparent black dots scattered on them.
- **Buds:** Crushing the buds will release a red substance, indicative of hypericin, a potent medicinal compound in the plant.

Medicinal Parts: The leaves, flowers, and buds are all imbued with medicinal properties.

How to Harvest: When harvesting, cut the flowers just beneath the bud to ensure you obtain the flowers, buds, and, if possible, some leaves.

Making Medicine:

- **Saint John's Wort Tincture:** Combine a handful of flowers, buds, and leaves with 1 ¼ cups of 50% alcohol.
- **Saint John's Wort Salve:** Take a handful of flowers (chopped or mashed) or utilize a simple oil. Combine with 1 ½ ounces of beeswax. Using a double boiler, heat the mixture on low to medium until the wax liquefies. Transfer the mixture into containers and let it cool.

Dosage: For the tincture, mix 1 teaspoon in half a glass of water and consume 3-4 times daily.

WARNINGS:

- Misidentification: One of the major concerns with Saint John's Wort is that it closely resembles Tansy Ragwort, also known as Saint James Wort. While Tansy Ragwort does contain some beneficial components, it also harbors potentially poisonous elements. Always be cautious and ensure you've correctly identified the plant.

Sea Buckthorn (Hippophae rhamnoides)

Plant Name: Sea Buckthorn

Plant Type: Stocky Thorned Shrub

Lore: Celebrated as a potent healer by the Tibetan people, the Sea Buckthorn has been treasured for its therapeutic properties for generations.

What Does it Treat:

- **Immune System:** Its rich Vitamin C content serves as an immune booster.

- **Respiratory:** It can provide relief for lung issues and respiratory disorders like colds and coughs.

- **Skin:** Sea Buckthorn has demonstrated efficacy in treating skin conditions, notably eczema.

Habitat & Region: These shrubs flourish in coastal hills.

Identification: A stocky and thorny shrub that can grow between 5-6ft in height, characterized by its dense, juicy orange fruit.

- **Flowers:** They bloom into modest green blossoms.
- **Leaves:** These are lanceolate, bearing a narrow and scaly appearance.
- **Fruit:** Its small, vibrant orange fruits cluster together.

Medicinal Parts: The primary medicinal components are the fruits.

How to Harvest: Harvesting the fruits demands caution due to the thorny nature of the shrub. Utilizing gloves and protective sleeves is a must to prevent injuries.

Making Medicine:

- Sea Buckthorn Oil: Combine 10oz of the berries with 3 teaspoons of alcohol in an 8oz mason jar and allow it to sit for 6 hours. Top it up with olive oil until the jar is full. Seal the jar and stir the mixture daily over a span of 3 weeks. Once the steeping process is complete, strain the mixture, and you're left with Sea Buckthorn oil.

- Salve for Skin Issues: To make a salve, mix 1-2 tablespoons of the oil with 1 ½ ounces of beeswax. This concoction is particularly beneficial for conditions like eczema.

Dosage: The oil can be applied topically as needed. For internal treatments, you can add 5-10 drops of the oil to a cup of tea. It's advisable to consume this 3-4 times a day.

WARNINGS:

- **Dosage Caution:** Like with any natural remedy, consuming large quantities can lead to side effects. It's crucial to adhere to the recommended dosage.

- **Allergic Reactions:** Some individuals may experience allergic reactions to Sea Buckthorn oil or any of its components. Always conduct a patch test before applying the oil extensively.

- **Pregnancy:** Pregnant or nursing women should consult their healthcare provider before using Sea Buckthorn as a remedy.

- **Lookalikes:** While Sea Buckthorn is relatively unique in appearance, always ensure correct identification before consumption to avoid ingesting a different and potentially harmful plant.

Skullcap (Scutellaria sp.)

Plant Name: Skullcap

Plant Type: Perennial Wildflower

Lore: Historically referred to as Mad Dog Skullcap, this herb has a longstanding tradition of being employed for mental health remedies, particularly for ailments like anxiety and depression.

What Does it Treat:

- **Sedative:** Skullcap has natural sedative properties, helping to induce relaxation and restful sleep.

- **Antispasmodic:** It's effective for relieving muscle tension and cramps.

- **Mental Health:** Its properties can be beneficial for mood improvement and stress reduction.

Habitat & Region: Skullcap thrives in moist environments like marshes and wetlands.

Identification: Bearing a resemblance to mint, Skullcap showcases multiple blue flowers sprouting from a tall, singular stem. Its tendency to grow in clusters makes it relatively easy to find in abundance.

- **Flowers:** Protruding from a central stem, these flowers droop downwards, spanning the entirety of the stem. They can vary in color, presenting shades of pink or even red.
- **Leaves:** Reminiscent of mint leaves, they can grow considerably larger in size.

Medicinal Parts: Both the leaves and the flowers are used for their therapeutic properties.

How to Harvest: The ideal time to harvest Skullcap is when it is in full bloom. Simply cut the plant at its stem.

Making Medicine:

- **Skullcap Hot Infusion and Tea:** Combine 1 tablespoon of Skullcap with 2 cups of water and steep for 10 minutes.

Dosage: Consume Skullcap tea 2-3 times daily to alleviate symptoms.

WARNINGS:

- Sedative Effects: Due to its inherent sedative properties, high doses can induce drowsiness and may lead to confusion. Caution is advised, particularly when driving or operating machinery.

- Lookalikes: Always ensure correct identification when foraging for Skullcap, as there are other similar-looking plants that might not have the same therapeutic benefits or might even be harmful.

- Pregnancy and Nursing: Women who are pregnant or nursing should consult with a healthcare provider before consuming Skullcap.

Slippery Elm (Ulmus Rubra)

Plant Name: Slippery Elm

Plant Type: Deciduous Tree

Lore: Revered in ancient Celtic mythology, the elm tree has deep connections with the underworld. Elves and goblins, believed to guard burial mounds, were often associated with or depicted near these majestic trees.

What Does it Treat:

- Respiratory Issues: Effective in alleviating sore throats and coughs.

Habitat & Region: Primarily found in highland woods or areas with rocky terrains.

Identification: Characterized by its medium stature, the Slippery Elm displays a mix of gray and red on its bark. The elongated trunk of the tree branches out extensively.

- **Flowers:** Unconventional in appearance, these "flowers" resemble fuzzy clusters that radiate outwards in a pattern similar to fireworks.
- **Leaves:** Pointy at the tips, these leaves widen towards the middle. With deep veins running from the center to the edges and a toothed perimeter, they're quite distinguishable.
- **Bark:** The distinctive bark of Slippery Elm is a mix of grey and red shades with deep, vertical grooves.

Medicinal Parts: The inner bark of the Slippery Elm tree is the primary source of its medicinal properties. This can be processed in various forms, like shreds or powders.

How to Harvest: To procure the inner bark, one can prune a few branches and strip the outer layer of bark, revealing the medicinal inner layer.

Making Medicine:

- Slippery Elm Hot Infusion and Tea: Mix 2 tablespoons of the inner bark with 2 cups of water and allow it to steep for 5 minutes.

- Slippery Elm Decoction: Combine 1 part of the inner bark with 8 parts water. Let this concoction simmer for at least an hour.

Dosage: It is advised to consume no more than three servings of the tea or decoction daily.

WARNINGS:

- **Interactions:** Slippery Elm can interfere with the absorption of certain medications due to its mucilage content. Always consult with a healthcare provider before using Slippery Elm, especially if you're on medications.

- **Pregnancy and Nursing:** It's essential to consult with a medical professional before consuming Slippery Elm during pregnancy or while nursing.

- **Lookalikes:** There are other species of elms. Always ensure you're correctly identifying the Slippery Elm to avoid mistakenly harvesting another species.

Staghorn Sumac (Rhus typhina)

Plant Name: Staghorn Sumac

Plant Type: Tall Shrub

Lore: Often referred to as the lemonade tree or vinegar tree due to its tangy berries which, when made into a drink, resemble the taste of lemonade.

What Does it Treat:

Astringent & Antiseptic: It has astringent and antiseptic properties beneficial for sore throats.

Immunity Booster: With a high Vitamin C content, it also serves to bolster the immune system.

Habitat & Region: Commonly found along the edges of deciduous forests.

Identification: Distinguished by its tall stature, the Staghorn Sumac can often be mistaken for a tree. During summer and fall, it becomes more recognizable due to its unique appearance.

- **Berries:** Known as drupes, these small, roughly ¼ inch berries cluster together, with each cluster holding between 100-700 drupes. These clusters resemble a horn, giving the plant its name.
- **Leaves:** Spear-shaped and alternate, they have a resemblance to the leaves of the black walnut.
- **Stems:** The newer stems are slender and green, while older ones turn dark brown, even nearing black as the plant ages.

Medicinal Parts: The medicinal attributes lie primarily within the drupe clusters.

How to Harvest: Peak harvest time is between mid-August to September in most regions.

Making Medicine:

- Staghorn Sumac Sun Tea: Fill a mason jar with the berries and cover with water. Place the jar in direct sunlight for 2-3 hours.

- Staghorn Sumac Tincture: A 1:3 mixture with 30% alcohol using the fresh berries.

Dosage:

- Sun Tea: Consume as per requirement.

- Tincture: Recommended dosage is 3-4ml, taken 2-3 times daily.

WARNINGS:

- **Lookalikes:** The most concerning lookalike is the Poison Sumac. Although the leaves of both plants may seem similar, Poison Sumac leaves are opposite and have a more rounded serration. Furthermore, the berries of the Poison Sumac are greyish-white, unlike the Staghorn's red drupes. It's crucial to be cautious and familiarize oneself with these differences to avoid accidental ingestion.

Thyme (Thymus vulgaris)

Plant Name: Thyme

Plant Type: Ground cover herb

Lore: In medieval times, thyme was believed to have protective properties, often being used as a remedy to overcome shyness.

What Does it Treat:

- **Antibacterial:** Thyme is renowned for its potent antibacterial properties.

- **Stimulates Blood Flow:** The herb is effective in promoting circulation.

- **Digestive Aid:** Thyme can assist with digestion.

- **Respiratory Aid:** For those suffering from congestion, thyme tea can be an excellent remedy to clear mucus from the membranes.

Habitat & Region: Often found in meadows and rocky terrains, sometimes growing against walls.

Identification: Its widespread use in cooking makes thyme a recognizable herb to many.

- **Flowers:** Small and delicate, the flowers can range in color from pink to lilac or even purple. They bloom from May to September, crowning the clusters of leaves.
- **Leaves:** These small, oval-shaped leaves, known for their culinary benefits, grow on thin woody stems, especially when the plant matures.

Medicinal Parts: Both the flowers and the leaves of the thyme plant have medicinal attributes.

How to Harvest: Use garden shears to trim thyme close to the ground for maximum yield.

Making Medicine:

- **Thyme Hot Infusion and Tea:** For every cup of water, use 2oz of thyme. Let it steep for about 10 minutes.

- **Thyme Tincture:** A 1:4 mixture using 30% alcohol, allowing it to sit for 4-6 weeks.

Dosage:

- Tea: It's recommended to have 2-3 cups of thyme tea daily.

- Tincture: Take 1 tablespoon 2-3 times a day for optimal benefits.

WARNINGS:

- **High Doses:** Consuming thyme in extremely high doses may lead to adverse effects like gastro-intestinal discomfort or headaches.

- **Allergies:** Some individuals may be allergic to thyme. It's always a good idea to test a small amount first or consult with a healthcare professional.

- **Lookalikes:** While thyme is quite distinct, there are many herbs with small leaves that may be mistaken for it. Always ensure proper identification before consumption.

Watercress (Nasturtium officinale)

Plant Name: Watercress

Plant Type: Groundcover

Lore: Legend from Denbighshire recounts a holy well from the 1960s where watercress thrived. Locals believed that this particular watercress could cure rheumatism, and it became so popular that it was sold door to door.

What Does it Treat:

- **Respiratory Ailments:** Acts as a remedy for bronchitis and congestion.

- **Allergies:** Some claim its consumption alleviates allergy symptoms.

- **Cleansing:** Watercress has properties that help in cleansing the body and can be beneficial for urinary tract infections (UTI).

Habitat & Region: Typically found at river edges, in ditches, and in shallow regions around cold running water.

Identification:

- **Overall:** A verdant groundcover with alternate dark green leaves and small white flowers when it's flowering season.
- **Flowers:** These are small, white, and bear 4 petals each..
- **Leaves:** Dark green in color, these leaves are set in an opposite arrangement. The topmost leaves are almost completely round.

Medicinal Parts: The leaves of the watercress plant are what hold its medicinal properties.

How to Harvest: It is best to use your hands or garden shears to pick watercress. Ensure you harvest before it starts flowering.

Making Medicine:

- **Watercress Hot Infusion and Tea:** Combine 2 teaspoons of watercress leaves with 1 cup of water, letting it steep for approximately 10 minutes.

Dosage:

- **Tea:** Consume the watercress tea based on necessity.

WARNINGS:

- Contamination Risk: Owing to the aquatic environment watercress grows in, it's often laden with parasites and bacteria. When harvested from the wild, it's essential to thoroughly wash and cook watercress before consumption.

- Lookalikes: There are other aquatic plants that might resemble watercress. Always ensure you're harvesting the correct plant.

Witch Hazel (Hamamelis virginiana)

Plant Name: Witch Hazel

Plant Type: Woody Perennial Shrub

Lore: Blooming around Halloween, the origins of its haunting name are a topic of debate, with no single explanation prevailing. The plant's late season bloom only adds to the intrigue.

What Does it Treat: Witch hazel offers a myriad of external applications. It can soothe and treat conditions such as poison ivy rashes, acne, burns, sunburns, eczema, gum inflammation, muscle aches, sprains, eye strain, bruises, insect bites, and more.

Habitat & Region: The shrub has a prolific presence across the eastern half of the US and is particularly adaptive to colder climates.

Identification: Recognizable by its distinct aroma, witch hazel has yellow flowers that manifest during the chilly seasons.

- **Flowers:** These unique yellow flowers look somewhat like twisted strands and can be found adorning the plant's branches from mid to late fall.
- **Leaves:** The simple ovate leaves have prominent teeth along their edges.
- **Bark:** The bark is of a smooth texture and has a greyish hue.

Medicinal Parts: Twigs, bark, and the plant's green buds are rich in medicinal properties.

How to Harvest: For the best yield, harvest during the fall. Dress warmly and carry a set of pruners for a smooth harvest.

Making Medicine:

- **Witch Hazel Fomentation:** Combine 1 cup of witch hazel (can be twigs, bark, leaves, or green buds) with 4 cups of water. Boil this mix, ensuring the vessel is covered, for about 20 minutes.

- **Witch Hazel Salve:** Melt 8oz of beeswax and mix in 1 tablespoon of chopped green buds or bark. Let this sit in a double boiler for a few minutes before straining.

Dosage: Apply directly to the affected areas as required.

WARNINGS:

- **External Use Only:** Witch hazel is primarily meant for topical application. Ingesting it can lead to stomach upset.

- **Potential Allergens:** As with any topical product, it's important to test a small patch of skin first to check for allergic reactions.

- **Lookalikes:** Other plants might resemble witch hazel, particularly during non-flowering seasons. It's vital to ensure you're working with the right plant, especially when aiming for medicinal use.

Veronica (Veronica officinalis)

Plant Name: Veronica

Plant Type: Perennial Herb

Lore: Belonging to the Speedwell family, Veronica is often referred to as the "green tea" of wild edibles, suggesting its prominence and favorability.

What Does it Treat: Renowned for its respiratory benefits, a hot infusion or tea made from Veronica can significantly alleviate cough symptoms.

Habitat & Region: This plant is predominantly found in meadows and prairies, frequently amidst forests or along old pathways.

Identification: At a cursory glance, Veronica may remind you of mint due to the similarity in leaf structure. However, its distinct baby blue, five-petaled flowers set it apart.

- **Flowers:** These are light blue with an almost white hue at the periphery.
- **Leaves:** They bear a striking resemblance to mint leaves — toothed at the margins, a sturdy central stem, and pronounced veins.

Medicinal Parts: Both the flowers and leaves serve medicinal purposes, particularly when used to brew tea.

How to Harvest: Harvesting Veronica mirrors the process for mint. Simply trim it and collect in bunches.

Making Medicine:

- Veronica Hot Infusion and Tea: Use 2 oz. of Veronica for 1 cup of water, and let it steep for about 10 minutes.

Dosage: Immerse yourself in the benefits of this "wild green tea" by consuming 3-5 cups daily.

WARNINGS:

- **Dose Moderation:** While Veronica is generally safe, it's always a good idea to consume in moderation and observe how your body reacts.

- **Potential Allergens:** Before consuming in large amounts, do a patch test or try a small amount to see if there are any allergic reactions.

- **Lookalikes:** As with many plants, there are similar species that may resemble Veronica. It's crucial to ensure proper identification, especially when the intent is medicinal or culinary use. Always consult with an expert or use a reputable field guide.

Violets (Viola sp.)

Plant Name: Violets/ Swamp Violet

Plant Type: Flowering low-lying plant

Habitat & Region: Violets are widespread across North America and can be typically found in wetlands and disturbed areas such as front yards.

Identification: This flowering plant is recognizable by its heart-shaped leaves and characteristic purple flowers that bloom between February and April.

- **Flowers:** Consist of five petals which could range from a vivid purple to an almost whitish-purple hue. The arrangement is such that there are two petals on the top and three below.
- **Leaves:** These are plump and heart-shaped, connected to the plant by fibrous stems.

Medicinal Parts: Both the leaves and the flowers are harnessed for medicinal applications.

How to Harvest: With a pair of kitchen shears, you can easily snip off some leaves and flowers.

What Does it Treat: Violets are renowned for their healing properties, particularly for skin irritations. They also exhibit anti-inflammatory qualities.

Making Medicine: The plant's properties can be accessed through a poultice, infused oil, or infusion.

- **Slimy Poultice:** Crush leaves and flowers to create a paste. This can be applied to affected skin areas.

- **Infused Oil:** Fill a jar with the leaves and flowers and cover with a carrier oil like olive oil. Leave in a sunny spot for 4-6 weeks, shaking occasionally. Strain and use.

- **Infusion:** Steep the leaves and flowers in hot water.

Dosage: The infusion can act as a mild laxative. Therefore, limit consumption to a maximum of 1 cup every 4 hours.

WARNINGS:

- **Excessive Consumption:** Overconsumption might lead to digestive disturbances due to its mild laxative effect.

- **Lookalikes:** There's a plant called Lesser Celandine which bears a striking resemblance to the violet but is toxic. It's imperative to differentiate between the two to avoid any adverse reactions. Always ensure proper identification and if in doubt, consult with a botanist or use a reliable field guide.

Wild Lettuce (Lactuca virosa)

Plant Name: Wild Lettuce

Plant Type: Grassy Herb

Lore: Wild lettuce has earned a reputation as a recreational herb, leading to its nickname, "lettuce opium", due to its sedative properties.

What Does it Treat: This plant is commonly used as a remedy for pain, respiratory issues, anxiety, and sleep disturbances.

Habitat & Region: Wild lettuce thrives in disturbed soils and can be commonly found in backyards.

Identification: Resembling the dandelion, wild lettuce can be identified by its purplish-green hue and its height, which can reach up to 80 inches.

- **Flowers:** They bear a striking resemblance to dandelions and are perched on thick stalks, along which you'll find the famed white sap that has lent to its "opium" nickname.
- **Leaves:** These leaves are adorned with thorns and should be avoided for consumption. **Sap:** The white, thick sap is one of the plant's distinctive features, and it's this sap that is often used to make tinctures.

Medicinal Parts: The plant's leaves, flowers, and sap hold medicinal properties.

How to Harvest: Arm yourself with a pair of small shears or pruners to harvest the plant.

Making Medicine:

- **Tea:** By drying and grinding wild lettuce, a tea can be brewed using 2oz per cup, which should be steeped for 10 minutes.

- **Tincture:** A ratio of 1:5 in 30% alcohol is recommended. A blender can effectively extract the sap. Subsequently, place the pulp in a vial to prepare the tincture.

Dosage:

- Tea: It's recommended to drink wild lettuce tea 2-3 times daily.

- Tincture: Administer 12-24 drops, 2-3 times a day.

WARNINGS:

- **Excessive Consumption:** Overconsumption of wild lettuce, especially in tincture form, can lead to dizziness, nausea, or more severe side effects. Always use in moderation.

- **Lookalikes:** Given its resemblance to the dandelion, proper identification is crucial. There are many types of Lactuca species; always ensure you have the correct one. If you're uncertain about the identification, consult with a botanist or use a reliable field guide before consumption.

Willow (Salix sp.)

Plant Name: Willow

Plant Type: Deciduous Tree

Habitat & Region: Often found in wetland forests and alongside creek banks.

Identification: Recognizable for their affinity for water, willows typically grow along water bodies. These trees tend to be bushy and feature slender, finger-like leaves.

- **Flowers:** The catechin-like flowers are compact.
- **Leaves:** Characterized by their simplicity and slender form.
- **Bark:** Mature willows exhibit thick, vertical ridges, while younger willows have smoother bark due to newer growth.

Medicinal Parts: Although willow leaves are rich in Vitamin C, the bark is more sought-after for its medicinal properties. It contains salicin, a compound that is a precursor to the active ingredient in modern-day aspirin.

How to Harvest: Employing a knife, pieces of bark can be taken from the trunk or larger branches. It's crucial not to remove the bark completely around the circumference of the trunk; doing so will harm the tree, potentially leading to its death.

What Does it Treat: With a history that spans back 4,000 years, the willow's medicinal benefits are well documented. Ancient Sumerian texts mention its use as a remedy. Willow is primarily known for alleviating fever and pain.

Making Medicine: Prepare a hot infusion using 2oz of willow bark and 1 cup of water. Store the harvested bark in a mason jar for future medicinal use.

Dosage: Consumption should be limited to 3-4 cups daily.

WARNINGS:

- **Overconsumption:** Excessive intake can lead to side effects like stomach problems or allergic reactions, similar to those caused by aspirin. Always consult with a healthcare professional before introducing any new herbal remedies.

- **Variety:** The White willow variant contains the highest concentration of salicin, making it more potent medicinally. Always be sure of your willow species.

- **Lookalikes:** There are many species of Salix, or willow, so proper identification is essential. Ensure you have the right species before harvesting or consuming.

Wintergreen (Gaultheria procumbens)

Plant Name: Wintergreen

Plant Type: Evergreen Shrub

Lore: In the 1860's homestead children were responsible for gathering up nuts and berries around the property. They would have been the ones to forage for wintergreen leaves and berries.

What Does it Treat: Fever, pain, and inflammation

Habitat & Region: Northeastern Mixed Forests or Pine Forests.

Identification: This evergreen shrub of the heath family begs for a dusting of snow. Its shiny green leaves and bright red berries look picturesque under a light dusting. This evergreen shrub is easy to identify when the berries are hanging.

- **Flowers:** Small whitish or pinkish flowers that bend and point downward.
- **Leaves:** Oval leaves are 1-2 inches long and leathery.
- **Berries:** The small red berries look similar to blueberries and huckleberries.

Medicinal Parts: The leaves and berries can be used to make medicine and they both contain the component methyl salicylate. This is similar to acetal salicylate which is a property of aspirin and has similar effects.

How to Harvest: You are after the leaves and berries. Both can be harvested by hand and stored in bags.

Making Medicine: Wintergreen Oil 1 cup of leaves to 4 Cups of a carrier oil heat slowly over a low heat for 10 minutes and then let sit to cool to room temperature. Strain leaves and bottle the oil. Great on feet or applied to temples when you have a headache. Also smells great!

Wintergreen tincture 1:4 40% alcohol or more. Store 6 weeks before use.

Dosage: Take 5 -15 drops of wintergreen tincture as needed.

WARNINGS (high dose dangerous, dangerous lookalikes)

Red berries that do not cluster are something you should get used to avoiding. Wintergreen is the exception to this rule. Though, you do not want to eat them by that handfuls because they have that methyl salicylate. They also have a texture that is spongy and not juicy. So, you will probably not want to eat them by the handful!

Be very careful with identification when it comes to these single red berries.

Yarrow (Achillea millefolium)

Plant Name: Yarrow

Plant Type: Perennial Herb

Lore: Renowned throughout history as a staple for soldiers, yarrow has been utilized to staunch bleeding on the battlefield.

What Does it Treat: Predominantly, yarrow is celebrated for its ability to halt bleeding.

Habitat & Region: Yarrow thrives at the fringes of deciduous forests and can often be found in residential yards and meadows.

Identification: Recognizable by its tall stalks, feathery leaves, and cluster of flowers at the top.

- **Flowers:** These composite flower heads bloom all summer and can manifest in shades of white, pink, or yellow.
- **Leaves:** : Finely divided, feathery leaves alternate up the stem, with the longest ones situated nearer the base.

Medicinal Parts: While the entire plant holds medicinal properties, the roots from mature plants (2–3 years old) are particularly potent.

How to Harvest: Ideally, harvest yarrow when the majority of its flowers, especially the yellow ones, are in full bloom. When collecting, bring along shears and a hori hori knife.

Making Medicine: To craft a yarrow styptic powder, suspend the stems and yellow flowers upside down to dry for a week or so. Once thoroughly dried, these can be ground using a mortar and pestle. This powder, when packed into a wound, acts as a natural coagulant and assists in stemming the bleed.

Dosage: In case of a wound, pack with the styptic powder, secure with a bandage, and apply pressure to aid in stopping the bleed.

WARNINGS:

- **Allergies:** Some individuals may be allergic to components in yarrow. It's crucial to test on a small patch of skin before extensive use.

- **Pregnancy and Breastfeeding:** Yarrow should be avoided during pregnancy as it can induce uterine contractions. If you are pregnant, nursing, or considering using yarrow for a child, consult with a healthcare professional.

- **Lookalikes:** There are plants, like poison hemlock, that may resemble yarrow. Proper identification is paramount to avoid toxic species. Always ensure you are harvesting the correct plant. When in doubt, consult a botanist or trusted field guide.

Yellow Dock (Rumex crispus)

Plant Name: Yellow Dock

Plant Type: Perennial Herb

Lore: Yellow Dock's multi-dimensional uses span from its inclusion in natural toothpaste formulations to its mystical associations with enhancing business and personal finances.

What Does it Treat: Yellow Dock is praised for its digestive-aiding capabilities and its potential in purifying blood. When crafted into a salve, it is also recognized as a potent wound healer.

Habitat & Region: Yellow Dock thrives in disturbed soils and pastures.

Identification: Distinguished by its tall flower-bearing stalk and slender curly leaves:

- **Flowers:** This plant boasts unique flowers devoid of petals, which adorn its tall stalks.
- **Leaves:** The lance-shaped leaves, with their characteristic wavy edges, are unmistakable.
- **Seeds:** Yellow Dock's seeds are enclosed in a papery sheath that turns a distinct brown, aiding in its identification.

Medicinal Parts: Of the entire plant, the root holds the most significant medicinal value.

How to Harvest: A hori hori knife will serve you well in digging up and accessing the roots without causing much damage.

Making Medicine:

- **Yellow Dock Hot Infusion:** For every cup of boiling water, use 2 oz of yellow dock. Allow it to steep for around 10 minutes before consumption.

- **Yellow Dock Tincture:** A 1:5 ratio with 30% alcohol is ideal. Once prepared, let the tincture rest for approximately 6 weeks in a location shielded from direct sunlight.

Dosage:

- For the tea, intake should be restricted to 2-3 cups daily.

- Tincture users should limit themselves to 15 drops, taken 2-3 times daily.

WARNINGS:

- **Oxalic Acid:** Yellow dock contains oxalic acid, which in high concentrations may lead to kidney stones or other kidney-related issues. Always consume in moderation.

- **Stomach Upset:** Some individuals might experience stomach upset or diarrhea. Cease consumption if these symptoms manifest.

- **Iron Absorption:** It can affect iron absorption in the body. Individuals with anemia or iron-related issues should use with caution.

- **Pregnancy:** Yellow dock should be avoided during pregnancy due to potential contractions and other related concerns.

- **Lookalikes:** Ensure you've identified yellow dock correctly, as there are other similar plants in the Rumex genus which may not have the same medicinal benefits or could be potentially harmful.

MAGIC LINGERS IN YOUR FINGERS

The Art of Plant Medicine

*"Mother Earth, lend me your strength, guide me
in your wisdom, and nurture my spirit as I*

Listen well, for we stand at the crossroads of age-old wisdom and the dawn of reawakening. For millennia, the bounty of nature, expressed in the form of medicinal herbs, has swathed civilizations with a nurturing green blanket of healing. Whether it's soothing a simple malaise, bolstering recovery from formidable ailments, or merely evoking a sense of deep-seated wellness, these earth-born potions have anchored human survival and fostered vitality.

Picture ancient times, a world where modern medicine was but a seed in the wind, and healing was cradled in the heart of nature. From the timeless gardens of China where herbal concoctions warded off the specter of maladies ranging from the common cold to the terror of malaria and tuberculosis, to the rich sands of Egypt, where botanicals served both the living and accompanied the dead in their mummification journey.

In the balmy heartland of Greece, Hippocrates, a patriarch of medicine, acknowledged the potent whispers of the plant kingdom, integrating their curative properties into his practice. And in the grandeur of Rome, gardens flourished with healing flora, their secrets revealed to those who knew to listen.

As the wheel of time turned, the Middle Ages saw herbal lore continue to weave its magic, though it was shadowed in the 19th century by the rise of modern medicine. But dear ones, the enchantment of natural healing is undying. Its allure contrasts starkly with the clinical coldness of traditional medicine, the latter reliant on synthetic aids and intrusive procedures.

Healing from the earth cradles numerous boons. It's a gentle kiss to your coin purse, with lesser side effects, and often a greater reach than prescription medications. Many of our green allies possess anti-inflammatory, anti-microbial, and anti-cancer virtues, and can bolster the body's defenses. Consider the warmth of turmeric, the zing of ginger, the pungency of garlic - all known for their anti-inflammatory properties. Echinacea and elderberry stand as sentinels, fortifying the immune system against trespassing infections.

In this age of technology and information, the forgotten wisdom of medicinal herbs is being rediscovered and revered anew. However, heed caution, for not all plants speak the language of everybody, and some may contradict with prescribed medications. Always seek the guidance of a knowledgeable healer before embarking on your herbal journey.

And, remember this - we are not the only ones who heed the call of the plants. Our animal kin too, from chimpanzees treating parasites with plants to elephants self-medicating with botanicals, and even birds using greenery to ward off illness, they all demonstrate the vital role of nature in health and survival.

So, dear reader, I leave you with this - plant medicine, interwoven into the very fabric of our existence, continues to nourish and heal us. The virtues of natural healing contrast starkly with the clinical coldness of modern medicine, boasting fewer side effects, economical costs, and a connection to the healing rhythms of the Earth. Yet always remember, nature's whispers must be heeded with knowledge and respect. The animal kingdom's affinity for plant medicine serves as a compelling testament to the importance and efficacy of natural remedies in sustaining health and survival. The power to heal is in your hands, or rather, your fingers. Reach out, and the magic awaits.

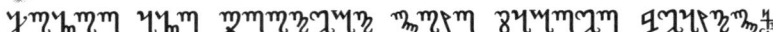

187

Printed in Great Britain
by Amazon

55979768R00110